BRIDGING THE GAP TO SOLVENCY

TO SOLVENCY

FIXING THE USPS

JOEL BENNER

PAGE PUBLISHING, INC.
Conneaut Lake, PA

First originally published by Page Publishing 2020

ISBN 978-1-6624-2325-3 (pbk)
ISBN 978-1-6624-2326-0 (digital)

Printed in the United States of America

Contents

Prologue

It is September 1st 2020 as Im writing this. Reading my memoir now, in a state of calm, the words portray someone who is in a state of stress.

The condition of the USPS reflects human nature set in an environment that rewards it. Job security, with opportunity has resulted in a robust amount of criminal activity. We have a library of OIG reports that reveals what is happening. It is over complex information that cannot be easily explained. The problem is growing exponentially.

Like all organizations that corruption finds its way into; there is a grooming phase for individuals who enter the USPS. Making "regular" is a good indication that an employee can be turned.

It was a freak occurrence of timing that produced this book. I expect lash back and will take it with humility and grace. Through writing an unfortunate experience I have found something I enjoy—Writing. I hope the public sees that our new Postmaster General is a man of integrity and to give him our unwavering support as he faces the herculean task of making our Postal Service self-sustaining.

Good luck sir.

The words you are about to read are my words and nobody else's. The words you are about to read bare consequence which I am prepared to take on alone. They are nonpolitical, they are based in the tenants of morality.

INTRODUCTION

Bestselling author Jerry Jenkins said, "Start with the good stuff." My dad could not see what my goal was for writing this book, and beyond the obvious of doing the right thing, he was right. So here it is.

In my late twenties, I made a series of poor decisions that resulted in bringing me to the brink of destruction despite my best efforts to resolve them. My marriage was destroyed; my business, my reputation—destroyed. I swore an oath to God I would walk a righteous path if he would give me another chance to regain what I had thrown away. So the purpose of this book is to enlighten the public, but it's also for myself. Would I have fallen in line with the individuals committing acts of malevolence if I had not lost it all before? Probably so. God's grace comes at the cost of holding my end of the bargain, and I will not go back to the depths of hell. None of this was enjoyable or fulfilling.

I had been a proud employee of the United States Postal Service for eighteen months when I wrote this book. I told myself I would write the entire book in nine days, the extent of my first vacation. I realized at twenty-five thousand words, it is too important to rush; too much is at stake. Great leadership is something that holds paramount value to ensure the well-being of the people within an organization. Corruption cannot be tolerated. Managerial problems cannot be ignored. Congress cannot solve the deep-rooted issues within an organization that employs 630,000 men and women. Only the American people can hold those responsible for the changes that must happen.

The postal service is a public service. It is the public tax dollar that will be spent on a 169 billion dollar deficit. The complexity of the situation can be understood only by experiencing it at the office level. I aim to bring factual events with known knowledge, building the bridge to solvency. Greed exists; it will always happen, and there will always be victims. I wrote this book based on my experiences to date as a postal employee. I specified my emotions and my opinions for readability and aiding in the likeliness that information entailed will become known by the public, inspiring action. The information is accurate. The names of the individuals have been changed. The purpose of this book is to not bring persecution and scrutiny on a few but to bring insight to those who possess the power to make real change. What makes the information entailed in this book valuable? It produces findings surrounding the effectiveness of laws designed to stop wrongdoing and protect whistle blowers against retaliation. Essentially, it is a case study. I have spent countless hours documenting what happened every day while at work. I did this because at some point, I would find myself in the position of convincing a man or woman that my unfortunate position was the result of dishonest people and not of my own merit. How would I do that? Record my history within the environment in as great of detail and accuracy as humanly possible. What's important to note: Virtually all post offices run the same way. An office in New York city performing a "wildcat strike" would roll over to other office on the opposite side of the country as displayed in the Postal Strike of 1970. Individual post offices are cells of a larger body.

Public support is the only cure. I invite you to enter.

CHAPTER I

Familiarity—Don't Worry, It's Only a Few Pages

The first question you will ask is how? Okay, I will tell you how. It probably is happening within the postal service. Given our financial position and years of unsuccessful intervention, it is plausible to assume there is more than what meets the eye.

Postal employees might be embezzling stamp stock.

I am guessing that it is not good enough; allow me to elaborate.

Imagine a lake being filled with water. On the other side is a drain. Our goal is to put more water into the lake being drained, yet the lake is not filling. That would suggest leaks, right? Imagine this lake was filled with sharks. The only way to find the leaks is by sending divers in the lake to look for them. Imagine the divers make it past the sharks and discover thousands of holes that could be leaks, but they cannot say for sure. The divers only know there is leaking somewhere. This is what we know.

Now the divers go back to a room full of manuals revised every two years over leaks. These manuals are five hundred pages thick and in a different language.

water = money
lake = postal system
sharks = employees
holes = different USPS revenue streams

There are 630,000 sharks that want the leaks to stop, just not at the expense of their shark food. A leaky lake with guaranteed shark food is better than fixing a lake with the risk of their shark food dwindling. The sharks see the water getting lower and lower but only care about the shark food right in front of them. The water continues to lower, and the sharks do not believe that it will run out.

shark food = benefits, pay, job, security

Okay, the above-stated information can be understood by 99 percent of the population. I will continue to go up in difficulty.

Postal Service Form 1412, daily financial sheet.

If Sally sells one book of seashell stamps, that is eleven dollars. At the end of the day, it goes on a PS form 1412 daily financial sheet.

It is entered by using a unique three-digit code known as an Account Identifier Code, or AIC.

AIC 007 is forever stamp sales.

The general ledger account number goes with the AIC, and corresponds to a financial reporting line where the AIC is located. The account number is eight digits long: 41110007.[3]

I'll just tell the story.

I joined the United States Army at nineteen. During my six years of service, I did two tours in Iraq. One was with the Tenth Mountain Division, Second Brigade Combat Team in the region known as the Sunni Triangle of Death,[4] and the other was in Baghdad, during the Iraqi presidential elections.[5]

In 2012, my military obligation was completed, and I loaded up a twenty-six-foot bed U-Haul along with my pregnant wife and headed back home to Ohio. Civilian life was an adjustment, and I tried a couple of different jobs before finding one I enjoyed. As a personal trainer, I experienced success, but after four years and 476 clients, I realized that it would be a wise decision to seek employment in a career that was long term and offered fantastic job security with a wide range of career-advancing opportunities. The United States Postal Service not only provided that but they also catered to veterans, which was icing on the cake. At thirty-one years old, I optimistically entered one of the largest workforces in the world. Six hundred thirty thousand employees collectively working together to accomplish delivering mail. A feeling of pride and excitement overcame me as I walked into the Powell Post Office on December 12, 2018, as the newest assistant rural carrier, ready to begin the learning curve.

On my first Amazon Sunday, I was paired with a young woman named Ayona. She did an awesome job of instructing. At every stop, she safely parked the Dodge Pro Master to the side, curbed the wheels to the right, shut the engine off, and exited the vehicle with the designated Amazon Parcel in hand. Upon exiting, Ayona ran to the door, placed the parcel on the porch, and ran back to the Pro Master. I thought, *Wow, what motivation.* Six hours and a van full of parcels later, we returned to the office. I approached my supervisor.

"How did it go?"

I replied optimistically, "It went great!"

Sharron gave me a smile and said, "Wonderful! Now I was not sure, but your paperwork has you down as a rural carrier assistant, but you said this morning you were an assistant rural carrier."

I asked, "What's the difference?"

Sharron replied, "Well, as an assistant rural carrier, you only work the weekends and rural carriers work all days of the week, so I went ahead and changed you to an assistant rural carrier status, but we need you, so go ahead and come in tomorrow!"

I said, "Okay, but I definitely want to make a career out of this if possible. Can I be a rural carrier assistant?"

Sharron smiled and said, "That's what we're hoping for!" On my way out, a man stopped me and introduced himself as Keith, the acting officer in charge, and wanted to know if I could come in early tomorrow, around 4:00 a.m. to spread parcels.

I replied with, "Yes, sir! I'll be there."

I worked in the Powell Post Office for an additional four months. I transferred somewhere closer. The Newark Post Office was one mile from my house.

I arrived at the Newark Post Office and approached the back doors. They were locked, so I rang the bell. A couple of minutes later, a gentleman answered the door. I informed him of who I was, and he introduced himself as Tim. Tim walked me over to the door to the left of the swinging doors. "Tomorrow, when you come in, enter a code on a keypad, and it will let you in: 1969."

Walking into the Newark office, I thought to myself, *This place is a lot larger than Powell.* Newark was a level 21 office. Newark had over forty city routes and fifteen rural routes. I had never seen a city carrier at that point in my career. The clerks on shift were Michelle, a taller woman in her late forties or early fifties who had started at Newark a week prior. Alaina was originally from Russia and had a heavy accent. Sam was a shorter guy who was the comic relief of the group; Sally was a woman who had been working for the Newark Post Office for over thirty years. She started when she was eighteen years old. And there was Tim, also a multidecade veteran of the Newark Post Office.

After introductions were made, our first truck arrived with the incoming mail. Jay had told me that he needed the parcels scanned by 8:00 a.m. The group energy was high. I observed my new coworkers closely to learn the process as fast as possible. The first thing to come off the truck were fifteen purple carts called FSS (Flats Sequence System) carts. Then there were DPS trays, followed by four large boxes on a skid composed of priority mail and first-class parcels. Once everything was staged in its appropriate place, we scanned under the PASS (Passive Adaptive Scanning System) machine.

"C-34, C-28, R-1, R-1," the robot voice called out the route numbers, and we made our way through the boxes. We averaged fifteen minutes per box; the average amount of parcels and flats per box was between 150 and 300 pieces.

At 5:15 a.m., a bell rang, and Alaina walked over to open the swinging doors. A taller gentleman entered, towing a skid of parcels. I asked, "Who is that?"

Sam said, "It is the truck driver from Amazon." The man brought in thirteen skids of Amazon parcels, one of which was a large box composed of bubble envelopes. It took an average of five minutes to complete one skid of Amazon. While the Amazon driver continued to tow in the skids, a woman wearing a USPS Sales and Service Associate shirt entered. Her name was Josie; she appeared to be well-kept and was not from the Newark area originally. Josie moved here with her daughters from out of state.

Around 7:15 a.m., men and women began to enter the building dressed as what I had always remembered as the stereotypical mailman appearance. The city carriers came in one by one. I recognized my mailman from my previous residence; C-26 was his route. At 7:59 a.m., we scanned the last of the parcels, and Sam shouted. "Parcels!" to inform all the carriers in the building that their hampers were ready to be taken to their cases and prepared for delivery. Alaina had the least seniority before me, so when it came to any questions I had, she was the one who told me what to do the first couple weeks.

After the morning parcels had been scanned, the next task was to sort the DPS mail onto shelf A. The average amount of time it required was thirty-five minutes.

At 9:30 a.m., the morning clerks headed to the break room to eat lunch. I sat facing the entrance door. Across from me was Sam; to his left, Sally. Josie sat to my right. At the adjacent table were Alaina; our postal one contractual clerk, Sid; and Tim. The topic for conversation that day was past PSE employees that had only been there for a short time. Sam told me there had been three in the last year. I asked why didn't they stay. He jokingly replied, "Alaina ran them all out."

Alaina said, "I did not run them out—you ran them out."

At 10:00 a.m., I saw Jay by the supervisor's desk and asked if he wanted to talk. It was the first time I had seen him since the day I walked in, seeking a postal service employee position a couple of weeks prior. He told me to give him a few minutes. Meanwhile, Michelle and Alaina had begun sorting the hampers to prepare for the incoming parcels that would be arriving at Newark throughout the day.

I walked over, and Michelle spoke to me. "I only been here for a week but Jay and I are friends. We know each other well. So what did you do before the post office?"

I replied, "Um, I actually was a personal trainer."

Michelle then told me she was a yoga instructor and taught classes on the weekend. The supervisor with Jay the day I came in beckoned me over to the office area. His name was Ted. Ted took me back to the postmaster's office and sat next to me. Postmaster Jay instructed me to have a seat.

Jay asked, "So what did you think this morning?"

"I was surprised. I didn't know what to expect, sir, but the floors were swept, and everyone was nice. It went well, I thought."

"What do you want to accomplish in the postal service?"

"Well, honestly, I want to be postmaster general. I know that probably sounds crazy, but I always believe if you set your goals high, you will end up somewhere in the middle."

"I wish I had ten more like you," said Jay.

A few additional minutes of introductions passed by, then Jay walked me back out to the main floor, where Alaina, Michelle, and Sam were finishing piecing back together the hampers.

We entered to the center of the workroom floor, where the closing supervisor's desk was on the adjacent side of the dispatch desk. Jay informed me that the dispatch clerk would be arriving in a few minutes, and he was to train me over the sales service dispatch associate position. His name was Bernie. Once Bernie arrived, Postmaster Jay took him off to the side and told him what I assumed the situation was about training me. Bernie was a nice guy, and we had our formalities. He was a middle-aged man, lean, and a hobbyist musician.

We set up the dispatch area, and Bernie walked me through the procedures of taking out the empty equipment the morning parcels arrived in a few hours prior. At 12:30 p.m., I approached Ted and asked if he had anything else for me, and he said I was free to go home for the day, to fill out a 1260 timecard, and that he would see me tomorrow.

The End of Civilities

The next morning, I came in the same way as before. I approached the door with the keypad "one-nine six-nine." The door did not open. The second day went similarly to the first. I met the third supervisor, Stacey, who was eight months pregnant and due to have her baby mid-June. The third day at the Newark Post Office was a Saturday. The truck arrived at 4:00 a.m., and we scanned parcels underneath the PASS Machine. At 5:30 a.m., the phone rang. Sam shouted, "There's Thelma calling off again!" I had not met Thelma at this point in time. Thelma entered work at 7:30 a.m. She was a well-put-together woman who recently transferred from West Virginia. She was the acting lead sales and service associate. A LSSA is the postal employee who oversees window operations and directly guides the window clerks who work alongside of him/her. The LSSA maintains comprehensive working knowledge of all postal products, services, and prices.

That following Sunday was my first day off at the post office. Monday, May 10, 2019, I arrived at the Newark Post Office and opened the door via code entry. Sam had injured his leg and called off work that day. There were three of us throwing parcels that morning—me, Alaina, and Michelle. Tim was in the case sorting letters alongside Sally. It was an adjustment compared to the first day I started with five clerks scanning parcels.

Volume that day was heavy. My instructions were clear, to have parcels sorted by 8:00 a.m. That Monday was the first break in hospitality as the tension began with Alaina shouting orders. If I had placed a spur (an item mailed inside a bag instead of the conventional cardboard box) inside a hamper instead of a tub, she would demand I place them inside the tub instead.

I was confused by the hostility surrounding the issue because whether the spurs were placed inside a tub or hamper, they were still going to the letter carriers' case to be sorted. As the carriers entered inside the building, we were on our last box of parcels. Josie had arrived and worked with us for a short amount of time but left to prepare for window operations. I threw a decent-sized spur inside a hamper, and I experienced my first real outburst from a coworker. After the spur landed in the hamper, I heard a shout. "Tubs! Tubs! *Tubs!*" I looked over at Ted and AJ. (AJ was a tall supervisor who began his career as a letter carrier.) To see their reaction to the break in manners, both sat and stared at their computer monitors. I did not respond to the outburst.

After completing morning parcels, I took the rural carriers back their hampers because where they were located, it was simpler if the clerks walked them over as they cased their mail. On my way over, Alaina demanded I go from case to case collecting misthrown letters (letters that had been placed in incorrect routes that required resorting). I did what she told me to do.

From 8:00 a.m. to 9:30 p.m., I was told to do multiple tasks by Aliana; it was mentally exhausting. I kept thinking, *What is going on here? This isn't how things went last week.* After lunch, we set up the hampers. The militaristic training continued.

Alaina said, "Look! You put six straps! Put four straps or parcels bounce out!"

(The USPS devised a new style of hampers that were designed to save the carriers' backs from strain. These hampers were blue and came with a bottom that was bungeed to the top and designed to descend as weight from the packages applied stress to the bungies. As the carriers removed parcels to be sorted, the bungies would elevate the bottom, preventing the carriers from repetitive bending.)

I asked, "Do you hear the way she is talking to me?"

"Only four straps, man," said AJ.

"I didn't put them like that," I replied.

"Yes, you did!" said Alaina.

After we finished placing the hampers in their respective places, I gazed toward Tim sorting red plum advertising mail (the coupon mailing that that people generally discard immediately). I walked over to help. I picked up a bundle of red plum and placed it down beside the carrier's case. "There you go. You help me, I help you. That is how that works. Oh, you should have heard Alaina ranting and raving you got Sunday off and she didn't." I looked at the schedule for the upcoming week, and it said that I would work Monday through Saturday, with Sunday being nonscheduled.

The following morning, we began working at 4:00 a.m. Josie came in around her usual time of 6:00 a.m. I asked her if she had any big plans for the weekend. She told me she planned on watching her son play baseball. Josie returned the question with, "How about you? Any plans?"

I replied, "Well, this Sunday, I'm going to go see my son and probably run some errands." Michelle interrupted. "You're working on Sunday." Certain that she misspoke, I said, "No, I'm working every single day this week." Michelle replied, "It has you on there, honey,"

Sure enough, Michelle was right. I continued to look over the clerk schedule to see if anyone else's schedule was like mine. The clerks all had two days off; I was the exception. I directed my attention toward AJ. "Come on, man, I need at least one day off a week. I have a kid." Michelle told me I had received my one day off. Michelle spoke genuinely. The way I was put on the schedule was to receive my mandatory day off a week at the beginning and end of the pay period, resulting in twelve consecutive working days. I am ashamed to say that is the first time I lost my composure as an employee of the USPS.

I shouted, "That's bullshit!" I expected some type of agreement among my peers; however, my expectations were shot down as I gazed upon three joyful clerks at the expense of my emotional response to my newly discovered work schedule. At that moment, I realized that civilities were a luxury I would not be so lucky to experience at the Newark Post Office.

CHAPTER 3

Battle for Environment

The following Sunday, I arrived at work, and Michelle was already there. Alaina had left instructions to be getting the PASS machine set up to scan parcels but had trouble getting the computer online. A supervisor from the town of Granville was the supervisor in charge that Sunday. We had mutual friends in the fitness world and spoke a little bit about the gyms in Newark. After the PASS machine became operational, Michelle and I scanned packages.

On Sunday, when Amazon was scanned, it was required to write the route number, followed by a number on the package. The number represented the order in which your stops were conducted. An example would be Y4-58.

Y4 = route.
58 = chronological stop

Michelle and I began talking.

"How do you like Newark?" I asked.

"The people here are so negative. The gossiping is awful. There was a rumor that I was sleeping with Jay."

"Why do you think it is like that?"

"Because they are jealous and want people to be like them, just negative all the time."

I did not comment.

The following Monday, I arrived at work at 4:00 a.m. Our completion time had progressively gotten later. Jay expressed how important it was to have the day's incoming parcels completed by 8:00 a.m. I wanted to do a good job. I picked up my pace in scanning under the PASS machine to the point where my heart rate was in an aerobics state.

I kept looking at the clock and back at the remaining parcels. The supervisors typically came in around 5:00 a.m. At 7:00 a.m., I felt a sense of panic if we still had a lot left. I picked up my pace again, scanning and running to the hampers or carrier cases. It was difficult because the morning clerks began standing in front of the read sensor, slowly scanning their parcels and slowly taking it to its appropriate place. I could not understand why they were doing this. I thought to myself, *This is a career job—why aren't they taking it seriously?* Asking this question would provoke an argument, so I did the best I could despite of the group workflow. The supervisors sat uninvolved at the desk, watching their monitors. We finished at 8:30 a.m.; at 9:00 a.m., it was time to collect the misthrown parcels (parcels tossed in the incorrect hamper and placed aside by the carrier who received it in error). As I went from case to case, I noticed the number of parcels misthrown was larger than usual.

My initial thoughts were that the carriers were just casing their mail faster, but as I collected three or four misthrown parcels from one case, he or she placed another to the side. I did my best to take the incorrectly placed parcels to the correct route; however, by 9:30 a.m., most carriers had departed for the streets. That Monday, the Newark Post Office had hundreds of parcels scanned out for delivery that were left behind due to being misthrown.

After lunch breaks were finished, AJ called me over. Two full hampers of misthrown parcels sat in front of him.

"Joel," said AJ, "we really need to focus on getting these parcels in the correct hampers."

"Do you think I am responsible for all of these?"

"Well, the clerks are saying you are."

After talking to AJ, I began to organize the hampers in the correct order. Behind me, I heard whistling and kissing noises. It was

Alaina. "Here, boy!" Offended by the gesture, I asked her to not whistle at me like a dog.

Once the hampers were set up, Jay walked out on the floor toward me. "Joel, next Monday, Bernie will be on annual leave. You are going to cover dispatch for him."

This made me overly excited. "Yes, sir!"

Jay continued, "Make sure you get more training in Thursday. Friday you are going to close with Bernie. He will take you through the process of the end-of-day dispatching tasks."

The next day, we carried out the morning parcel scans as usual. Once the letter carriers left the building, instead of collecting misthrown mail, I went to the dispatch area to begin setting everything up to practice the dispatch procedures. A few moments later, Sally approached. She spoke authoritatively. "What are you doing! We do not do this. Get over there!" She pointed to the post office box section.

I felt an urgency to learn the dispatch setup. I chose to ignore her and carry on with setting up.

"Oh yeah! Okay! No problem," said Sally.

I focused intently on the diagram Bernie had drawn the day prior. I knew I had seconds before a supervisor would approach me and cease what I was doing. I got halfway through the setup before AJ echoed Sally's command.

Thursday, May 16, 2019, was my day off. That Friday, I would be working a split shift so I could learn the dispatch closing routine. After the morning parcel scans were completed, a new record of misthrown parcels would be set. I shockingly gazed upon two hampers overflown of parcels that were scanned out for delivery. Stacey and AJ got everyone in the immediate area's attention.

Stacey said, "We have way too many misthrown parcels, you guys."

Alaina spoke abruptly with her heavy Russian accent more pronounced than usual. "Yesterday, we had only fifteen parcels misthrown!"

My jaw hit the floor.

Stacey said, "Joel, you need to make sure you are getting the parcels in the correct hamper, even if that means slowing down."

I tried to speak, but the words would not come out. I departed at 11:00 a.m. and was due to be back at 3:00 p.m.

Upon returning, Michelle approached me. "I just want to let you know that Tim went through the hampers yesterday and sorted any parcels that had been misthrown before they were given to the carriers for delivery. Tim sorted them while the other clerks scanned them under the PASS machine."

Michelle put in her two weeks' notice that day.

Bernie took me through the various dispatch duties. He was a good guy and highly informative. That is where I met Luke. He was the closing supervisor and the first person I met who acknowledged any performance conducive to the postal mission. Words of affirmation are so empowering and so easy to give, yet they are rarely given. When multiple people say something negative toward you, the belief that it is true sets in. If Michelle had not told me what Tim did the day before, I would have gravitated toward the possibility I was misthrowing parcels that resulted in a delay of mail. The reason of them doing that was to demean the intensity that I worked with recklessness. When things are said by multiple people, the possibility of doubt dwindles by a full magnitude. Witnesses serve credibility in court cases because its validating what is being said. The clerks begged the supervisors to let me go before I had reached the end of my ninety-day probationary period. The only reason I survived was that Jay needed an office that functioned and I was his best shot. Jay was the man that protected me. Everyone told him to let me go. I drove on with duties that needed to be completed.

As the carriers returned from their routes, I felt a great sense of pride in seeing their return. I almost wanted to give each one a hug as they returned from a long day walking the chaotic streets of Newark, Ohio, a town once generally free of homeless and drug abusers, now littered with those who have fallen victim to the results of addiction. The United States letter carriers are beacons of light in the darkest of areas. Through rain, sleet, snow, or wind, the backbone of our iconic organization. They do not falter; they will not stop. The mail must go through.

Saturday was my first day on dispatch by myself. I set everything up in accordance to Bernie's chart. I put the placards on the appropriate containers, separated by section. The postal service uses a placard system to separate different classes of mail.

1. Media mail—DVDs, magazines, books, or reading material. Sound recordings.
2. Library mail—this class can only be used for mailing books or educational material to and from libraries, museums, etc.
3. Retail ground—we typically use this if the container has a product that cannot go on airplanes or exceeds 108-inch length and girth.
4. First-class package service—this is the most economical choice for people mailing small items. It can't weigh over 13 oz.
5. Priority mail—This is our bread and butter.
6. Priority Mail Express—one to two days, real fast, real expensive.

Let us say Jessica on City Route ten handed me a parcel; the first thing I would do is look at the postage insignia or the sticker that says the price paid. I see the sticker has a *P* on it. I know its priority. The next thing I would look at is the zip code: 78701. I know that is Austin, Texas, and would be placed in the 04 containers. There are nine total containers at the start of a dispatch shift. At the end of the day, a truck from the processing plant arrives to pick them up and transports them back. At the processing plant, they are run through a machine on a conveyer belt that sorts them again to be taken to a specific location where they are loaded on a truck and transported to the airport to be flown to the next processing plant closest to the address of the receiver. Once arrived at the processing plant, the parcels are offloaded, sorted a final time, and sent to the dock of the appropriate truck to be transported to the receiver's local post office. The morning clerks would take the parcel and scan it under the PASS machine, letting the receiver know it is out for delivery and they should expect it the same day. Time is of paramount importance in the USPS. Everything is a race against the clock. Teamwork and communication are essential for smooth deliveries.

Once everything was set up, it was time for me to collect the parcels at the window clerk station. Once collected, I sorted the parcels in their correct location. I ate lunch, and for the first time since I had started at Newark, I found myself with nothing to do for a couple of hours. Looking around, I noticed the floors were filthy and trash cans overflown with garbage. One of our custodial staff members had just retired a few days earlier, and Mike, our other custodian, was on annual leave.

I walked to the janitor's room, where all the cleaning supplies were located and grabbed a mop and filled the mop bucket with water. I began mopping at the rear of the building near the back offices and worked my way up toward the front. I completed most of the main workroom floor before the carriers returned from their routes. After the end of my dispatch duties, I asked Luke if there was any word on the status of our paychecks as they had not come the week prior. He did not answer. At that point in time, I was down to my last few dollars. The combination of a mandatory six days off from the transfer from Powell to Newark (when postal workers switch job titles, they must have a layover period of six days) and the delayed paychecks had resulted in nearly a month with no income.

I asked Luke if he could give me an idea of how much my paycheck would be. Luke pulled up my pay period for the days I had worked. He read off my hours. An entire day was missing from the paycheck I had not received.

Sunday, May 19, 2019, I arrived at Newark Post Office to prepare for Amazon Sunday. Stacey was the supervisor in charge that day. She was wearing sweats with her pregnant belly sticking out. It was Michelle, me, and Alaina. Alaina had not shown up yet. Michelle and I started with the Amazon parcels, and Stacey walked over to assist us. I was concerned because I did not want her to hurt her baby. I remember being overly cautious that day. Stacey talked about her family a little bit and how she came to America when she was only eight years old. She told us that her brother was a postmaster. I worried about Alaina and asked Stacey if she had called her? She was a heavier-set girl, and I worried my coming to Newark made her feel set back. I assumed that the contention beginning to manifest was due to insecurities or desires to maintain control of the environment. Alaina had been at Newark for over a year when I came, and I could see how someone like myself could be discouraging to an individual trying to progress in her career, especially being a foreigner. I just did not want her to feel any hopelessness for life. Aliana showed up a few minutes later, and I felt a sigh of relief. After the Amazon parcels were scanned, Stacey received a phone call of a carrier calling off. I volunteered to fill in as a parcel runner. Switching from an assistant rural carrier to a postal service employee, I was proficient at delivering Amazon parcels. I finished around 4:00 p.m.

The following day I arrived at the Newark Post Office; it was absolute chaos. I was scheduled split shifts all that week: 4:00 a.m. to 8:00 a.m., 1:00 p.m. to 7:00 p.m. There was a leadership team in the office that week. I am not positive who they were, but it became obvious that the morning clerk staff was deliberately underperforming during their visit. The only reason I could postulate to why they indulged in such behaviors was to embarrass Jay. I had heard the supervisors speak of the Union and how it limited their ability to do their jobs. I wanted Jay to succeed. I felt he deserved a chance. I wanted the new supervisors to have a platform to develop themselves and do great things within the postal service. I would not let these people destroy that. I would not conform to that malevolence. I would gather every ounce of strength I possessed to make sure the Newark Post Office was the absolute best and we set the standards of excellence within our organization.

I left for my four-hour break at 8:00 a.m. I came back at 1:00 p.m. The office was obliterated. It looked like a bomb had just exploded. A line of blue hampers lay from the PASS machine to the swinging doors. The supervisors were all inside the back offices with the management team. I felt scared for Jay. I thought of the consequences that would come his way if anyone saw this nightmare sitting here for hours. The morning clerks were nowhere to be found. I looked at the clock and said to myself, *One hour to get this done. Go.*

I started with the hampers. I arranged all sixty in the correct order around the PASS machine. Next, I started on the empty BMEs from the morning, loading them in the truck. I taped placards in their appropriate location on the dispatch BMEs that would be used to transport outgoing mail according to class; I pushed the BMEs filled with parcels from the front window to the dispatch area, unloading the parcels inside to the appropriate dispatch BMEs that would soon be in transit to the processing plant. The leadership team exited the office. Covered in sweat, I looked at Jay and gave him a thumbs-up, in which he returned the gesture. I felt confident and motivated as if we were in this fight together. There is always a tug of war between good and evil. We would prevail not only for our organization but for the amazing carriers that walked the streets of the struggling town of Newark. We would prevail.

The following morning, I arrived at the Newark Post Office. It was 3:55 a.m.; I was the only one there. At 3:57 a.m., I saw headlights, and it was Alaina's car. She exited, and I asked, "Where's everyone at?"

Alaina replied, "I do not know."

Sally came shortly after. Upon entering, I clocked in, and the first truck arrived. I knew today would be a tough day. The parcel's volume was particularly heavy, and it was only Alaina and myself as the scanning clerks. She gave it everything she had. I saw through Alaina, and I saw her heart. It made me sad to think that much of the way she had been acting was the way she felt she had to, to excel or feel safe in the environment. I took much of the tongue lashing I received from her with compassion and understanding. We finished the parcels at 9:00 a.m.

I had to leave to be back for my split shift. Like the day before, nothing was completed. It was a Groundhog Day of the day before. At 4:00 p.m., the carriers started returning from their routes. Luke had been dealing with complaint after complaint. The post office floors were light brown from dirt that accumulated on the floor due to weeks of negligence. The trash cans were flooding over. On the far side of the post office was the UBBM (undeliverable bulk business mail) section with weeks of pileup. Luke was the only supervisor there. Order was slipping away, and the gradual decline of duties began to appear obvious. No one enforced anything. The supervisors didn't appear to be concerned and really lacked any intervention. It appeared that Jay and myself were the only two people that desired to do our jobs well and fulfil the postal mission. I studied Luke's body language, and his physiology started to change. With multiple complaints, Luke's appearance turned pale and helpless.

I had to do something drastic. The office was on the brink of collapse. People feed off group energy. That's why when negative events happen in group settings; it's at a gradual decline leading to a collaborated effort to induce change. It always is chaotic and costly to the organization. At 6:30 p.m., the final dispatch truck departed. Luke finished his end-of-day duties and locked everything up. He asked if I was okay. I told him I would lock the small gate before I leave. Luke left the office defeated. I stayed and gathered all of the energy I had within myself. We would get through this. We were the Newark Post Office.

I stood in the middle of the dispatch area. I began looking around, gazing at the dark, filthy office. I had been up since 2:30 a.m., and I saw carrier after carrier display their frustrations. I felt responsible even though I was not. To have the people that faithfully march the streets every day return to disorder was unacceptable to me. To have supervisors unable to focus on problem-solving and personal development was unacceptable to me. If I felt able, I would intervene. The pride of a United States postal worker and the desire to uphold the conduct and standards of one of the longest-running organizations in history set fire upon my soul. It was as if a shot of adrenaline had been administered in my body.

There were thousands of parcels due to be delivered tomorrow morning. Thoughts of going home entered my mind as I stared at the behemoth amount of work that had to be completed before eight o'clock tomorrow morning. I shook the thoughts away and forced my legs to start moving, I was listening to a guitar player named Rob Joyce, whom Keith Urban called up on stage at one of his concerts.

I started scanning: C-34, C-29, R-12, R-2. My mind went to the guitar player and the shock on Keith Urban's face; I thought about what emotions he could have felt. What emotions the guitar player could have felt and what those five minutes did to the way he viewed the world. Would he come out of it better or worse? Would he feel entitled? What risk comes into play when you let strangers enter your ORA? I think so much of damage done from one person to another is unintentional, but to expect that someone will behave appropriately to something that is a gesture of kindness can be too much to ask for; however, in this case, the guitar player conducted himself as a gentleman.

The clock read 9:00 p.m., and my consciousness went back to my physiological state, and exhaustion consumed me. I needed to find that source of dopamine. How could I organize my thoughts to keep on going? I looked at the UBBM pile ignored for weeks. I pictured the carriers coming in on the brink of a meltdown expecting hardships only to find relief and a boost of hope to carry on the important postal mission. I forced my legs to move. I sorted through the junk mail and searched for another place to take myself while I worked. I could not find anywhere other than what importance I was doing. I held on the readiness of our office. As the time passed, so did the opulence of my delusion. I finished the UBBM.

The clock struck 10:00 p.m., and the time since I clocked out had long passed. The floors were filthy. It had bothered me since day 1. Anxiety often came to me by the dirt on the floors. It should not be there. A professional establishment as great as the USPS must have clean floors. That is the first thing people see when they walk in. Cleanliness improves efficiency and presents professionalism. How could the management staff of Newark take control if the place was a disaster? No one would take them seriously. Pride in the importance of what we were doing was paramount. We had to come together as a team. I began by sweeping the entire workroom floor. The amount of dirt and garbage filled half of a fifty-five-gallon trash can. Next, I mopped. I changed the mop water seven times; it became mud after a few passes. Once the mopping was complete, I departed for home.

It was 11:20 p.m. Tired, manic, and slightly delusional, I sent the management team this text:

The following day was Friday, May 31. I woke up at 7:37 a.m. I sat up in bed, running the memories of last night in my head. It closely resembled the feeling one gets when they reflect on a drunken night out, embarrassed at how they behaved the night before. I thought to myself, *I can't believe I did that.* I texted Ted to see if our paychecks had arrived. The three bubbles appeared on my phone signifying a response was formulating. "Yes."

I immediately drove to the Newark Post Office. I wanted to deposit my paycheck before my shift began. It was quiet walking in. The carriers were casing, but the typical sound of hustle and bustle was absent. The only thing that could be heard were envelopes shuffling against each other and mailbags being packed. The supervisors stared blankly at the computer screens. I stood there for a few seconds before I spoke. "Umm, can I get my paycheck real fast?"

Ted snapped out of his frozen state and shuffled through the large envelope they arrived in. "Here you go." Ted handed me the check. I felt so much relief. I made my way toward the door.

I deposited my check and returned with time to spare before clocking on. I went to the break room and started reading a book called *The Fault in Our Stars* by John Greene. It was a book about a teenage girl living life with cancer. I read about half of it. It made me feel sad.

Tim walked in, and I could tell this was the beginning of today's storm. Body language says far more about someone than the words that come out of their mouth, "Joel! Hey, what time did you leave last night?" Tim was notorious for filing grievances, and because I was a PSE, he could take the hours I worked, and the post office would compensate him for those hours. It is a complicated system that does not make a ton of sense, but it's postal law.

"Um, normal time…"

A look of fury came across Tim's face. "The damn floors were wet when I came in!"

I did not respond.

Tim continued, "That's okay! I'll pull the clock rings."

Tim was the Union representative of the Newark Post Office and had the right to pull clock rings to see when people clocked in and out. I clocked out at my ten-hour mark but worked for free. I had been at the post office for sixteen hours the day prior.

Thelma walked into the break room. "Oh, you're Joel, aren't you? There's a lot of people talking about you."

I gave an awkward smile. "Oh, yeah? Good or bad?" I started my shift and removed empty BMEs to the trailer. I had to use the restroom, so I made my way over to that direction. I passed by the morning clerks.

Alaina said, "You come mop my floor!"

AJ said, "You guys are just mad he's showing you up."

I thought, *Oh god, do not say that.* At noon, UPS arrived and wheeled in two carts filled with bags of parcels to be scanned. I emptied the bags into a box to be taken over to the PASS machine. I looked over and noticed AJ was writing numbers on transparent pouches, the type of pouches that a school-aged child would put their pencils in. Later that day, AJ started putting the Arrow keys in these pouches (the Blue USPS mailboxes and apartment complex mailboxes are opened by what is called an Arrow key. Every mail carrier is assigned one to his or her route. This key is an accountable item, and if one is lost, every USPS mailing box that requires one must have the locks replaced). I found this perplexing because there were four Arrow keys missing from our assigned Arrow keys lot, which is beyond unacceptable. If I had to analogize, I would compare it to having a nuclear turnkey missing from the pentagon. At that point in my career, however, I did not know the magnitude of the violation. I knew it was an accountable item and the need to protect myself was prevalent. After the carriers had returned and the outgoing parcels had been dispatched, I handwrote a paper documenting the missing Arrow keys. I asked Luke to sign a paper confirming they were missing before I began employment at the Newark Post Office.

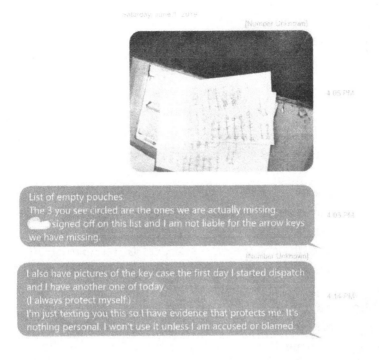

On Monday, June 3, I was back to my regular morning schedule. I entered the building at 4:00 a.m. At this point, my sympathetic nervous system activated upon arriving (fight or flight). I knew this was a problem because the response became automatic. It would produce a sustained level of cortisol released in my bloodstream. It would begin to deteriorate my body and, more importantly, my brain functioning. I had just celebrated my 32nd birthday, and quitting the USPS was not something I wanted or was willing to do. The mitigating factor between my legacy as a man, a father, a potential mate, and the credibility of my character lay in my ability to solve the inherent problem of my environment. I had three options:

1. Conform to the groupthink behavior of my peers, which would inevitably be counterproductive and destructive to the postal service.
2. Quit the postal service, which would be the end of Joel Benner, because at thirty-two there are no more excuses for

a man not "having it together." I would be forever known as a degenerate war veteran who suffered the empirical life defects of combat and should be pitied and deemed a burden to society.

3. Fight my way out of hell, become a dynamic factor in providing Jay with a functioning post office so he can reward performance, embrace the spoils of excellence, and train the supervisors to be great postmasters.

Great leadership would be the cure, a vaccine of hope to a historical organization nearly at collapse. My only path forward was straight ahead.

I clocked in at 4:00 a.m., and parcels were particularly heavy that morning. My entire focus was hitting the completed time of 8:00 a.m., just finish the parcels by 8:00 a.m. The only plausible explanation I could think of why the clerks were going to such lengths to prevent order and performance was control of their environment. It was a power struggle between them and Jay. The lack of intervention between the supervisors was a mystery. Ii couldn't figure it out; it seemed so simple and baffled me. With leadership comes conflict if the subordinate is deviating from the environmental goal. The only environmental goal present should be conducive to the postal mission. That was the only thing that made sense; it was the only thing that would yield an all-around fulfilled environment. The post office was paying our bills. I tried to reason with the supervisors, asking them to just talk to us in a group and give goals, guidance, challenges—something to strive for and keep our minds positive. The response I often received was, "The Union makes it impossible." I didn't believe it. It wouldn't be hard to set goals and incentives for effort. Even if it was a pizza day or a certificate.

We finished the parcels at 8:20 that day. I spread the DPS letters.

During the spreading, Alaina got my attention. "Pssst, come over here and help with spreading parcels."

After morning parcels were completed, we would transport the scanned parcels to the rural route side of the workroom floor.) I

34

refused because the carriers had to be out the door by 9:00 a.m. After the carriers had left, the clerks and I went to lunch.

After we returned from lunch, I received a text message from AJ. "Hey, man. We are getting a lot of issues with DPS. When you put it up, it needs to be right. There were two carriers Thursday had to come back today because the DPS trays were mixed up. The carriers do not have an extra twenty minutes to waste doing that."

"Yes, I thought that was strange too. I had to go back and fix two carriers DPS. Tim told Alaina to tell me to stop doing DPS and to help with misthrows, which raised red flags. There was also a stack of DPS in a strange area (the shelf cart) hidden with the cage up. I did a walkaround and did a quick look around. I'm a smart guy, and I've never had problems matching numbers. I cannot tell you with 100 percent certainty I made no mistake, but I highly doubt it. I will tell you from now on I will reassure management behind my duties that way if an issue comes up again, we can narrow down why it is happening. My counting my misthrows seemed to eliminate that problem. I am assuming so will this.

"Off the record, If there is any possibility, it could be from an individual rather than my negligence? I would ask myself, 'Why would someone do that?' I will tell you one thing I am not doing anymore is sharing openly with my peers the hours I am assigned to work. Could that cause grief for some people? I always look for patterns.

"On the record, I am sorry. I will try to improve."

AJ said, "You threw the DPS. There were trays of C16 and C18 mixed. Just pay closer attention. When I do it, I look at each tray label."

"I will. If there is anything I can do to rectify the matter, please let me know. It will not happen again."

"Just look at tray labels. Not a big deal. I appreciate your willingness to correct potential issues."

I began seeing a trend. Why would management want me to make mistakes? I was less than forty days in my career as a PSE. I went above and beyond to complete work that they were responsible for ensuring its completion. I wanted them to trust me and know we are on the same team. Why didn't they?

Returning from lunch, I made my way toward the PASS machine area and began setting up the hampers. I scanned FedEx parcels along with the meds from the VA. UPS arrived shortly after and offloaded their parcels to us. I scanned them at 11:00 a.m. Alaina scanned until she hit her eight-hour mark, and then I was by myself.

At 3:00 p.m., I had to leave. I hated leaving parcels for the next morning but had no choice, Sid our postal one had watched over my hours, also a utilizer of the grievance system. I went home and took a nap. I woke a couple hours later, feeling restless. We had to get ahead. I was tired of playing catch up. I did not care what it took I would work sixteen hours a day if that is what I had to do. I drove to the Newark Post Office around 5:00 p.m.

Sid spotted me. "Joel, what are you doing here?"

"Oh, I just forgot something, Sid."

I scanned around 245 parcels before Sid caught wind. He became furious. *"You better not be working off the clock!"*

I exited without further communication.

Mike was still on annual leave, and the grass at the Newark Post office was knee-high. If it did not get cut, the city would cut it and send us a bill.

Jay approached. "Hey, would you be willing to cut the grass? We got to get it done."

"Yes, sir!" I said. "When do you want me to do it?"

"Tomorrow morning, come in at 8:30 a.m."

I didn't know what to think when it came to the clerks. It had been carnage the entire time I was at Newark. I assumed the maintenance man James would not allow me the use of the postal mower. He had already stopped me when I emptied an overflowing trash can, saying that I needed to be careful over something called *cross crafting*. The following day, I brought my own lawnmower and cut the grass.

The following two weeks would be a paralyzed storm of conflicts between June 5 and June 21, 2019. The burglary alarm was triggered, and Tim, along with Sam and Sally, went to AJ, claiming

I had done it. Mike was back from his annual leave, and I could not work with debris on the floor. I swept every day, and Mike said something to management every day.

I finally asked about the cross-crafting issue. It was explained that it was put in place to protect the jobs of the contractual employees. Management could not do any contractual employee labor, and an employee had to stay within the work stated in his or her position. I did not understand the explanation. How could I threaten a peer's job for doing duties they didn't do?

The climactic event of my time as a PSE was a verbal assault that took place on the work room floor. It was a little after 6:00 a.m. Sam and I had been performing the morning scans when the Amazon driver arrived. I assisted the driver in unloading the truck when a unit fell over. I picked the scattered parcels off the floor.

Josie walked in the building. "*Get your fu——in ass over there and scan parcels!*"

"Excuse me?"

"Shut the f——ck up and do what you're fu——ing told!"

"You don't listen!" said Sam.

I heard three different voices come at me in all different directions; it was absolute insanity. I left for the break room and called AJ.

"Hello?" AJ responded.

"AJ! The clerks are freaking out. They are cussing me out. What do you want me to do?"

"Okay, just stay in the break room until I get there."

I hated that my peers were so disgruntled. I believed in Jay, I believed in the postal mission and there was no reason I could see that suggested I withhold completing tasks that must be done to a standard clearly instructed. They had to be done.

CHAPTER 4

A Terrifying Possibility

June 26, 2019, was the day I met Louise. Louise was the sister-in-law of a former supervisor, now postmaster who came to the Newark Post Office as our new T-7. The first time I saw Louise was on a Saturday. Bernie was off on the weekends, and I did the Saturday dispatch. Her brother-in-law stayed with her on the first day. After I finished sorting the outgoing parcels from the window, I saw Louise walk into the women's restroom always ten minutes before the lobby closed. I made my way over to the PASS machine and scanned FedEx parcels. Louise approached me and assisted in the parcel scans. She engaged in arbitrary conversation with me in which I gave arbitrary responses: "Do you have any kids?" "How long have you been with the post office?" etc. The man she brought with her would tell me more about this individual than she could in meaningless chatter. I watched his body language because I was not speaking directly to him; his expressions would reveal why he was there. The way he watched me was a cautious gaze. I ceased chatter with Louise.

"What's up, man?" I asked. "Who are you?"

"I used to be one of the supervisors here. I'm a postmaster now," said the brother-in-law.

"What's it like being a postmaster?"

"It's just like running your own business."

A few hours later, I looked up Louise on social media. She had posted pictures of herself and her brother-and-law toasting in celebration. The question was, what were they celebrating?

On July 1, Alaina was due to return from window training. It was an exciting time for her because she would finally become a regular employee. A regular employee in the USPS was when you became a career employee. You receive all the benefits and job security generally known within the USPS. Some employees go years without making regular, and it was a great achievement when it happened. I saw Alaina and went over to congratulate her; that is when she told me she had failed. Seeing the sadness in her eyes, a feeling of nausea overtook me.

Alaina did not fail. She was failed. Why would anyone fail an intelligent bilingual woman for a customer service position? It was a waste of time, money, and effort. Detestable, inexcusable. Abysmal! *Unacceptable!* So many words came to my mind. My light came on and knew from that moment what was going on. I had a canvas. My mind would paint a picture. My thoughts screamed, *You will not derail people's lives!* I followed her response with a line of questions. She was surprised because I generally try to be as subtle or hide my emotions.

"What was your test score?" I asked.

"They did not give test scores," said Alaina.

"What do you mean they didn't give you a test score?"

"It's only pass or fail."

"What's your teacher's name?"

"Michelle."

"What's her number? Give me her number right now."

"*No!* Why'd you want her number?"

I regained my composure.

Major predictors of long-term life success are the following:

1. Fluid IQ—the ability to solve new or novel problems and identify patterns.
2. Industriousness—constantly, regularly, or habitually active or occupied.

3.   Consciousness—The quality of wishing to do one's work
     or duty well and thoroughly.

When people high in these traits develop personal agendas is
the moment real danger becomes prevalent. If I truly worked for the
USPS, then I would be a problem to anyone that worked for themselves within the USPS. It would be a battle to survive. "Kill or be
killed" for lack of better words. The danger of a destroyed reputation
discredited and blackballed in society.

I could never teach my son the importance of virtue if I turned
around and inflicted pain onto people because doing so would provide an easy path forward. I completely bought the "union spiel." It
fit, it made sense, and that's what the dysfunctionality appeared to
be credited to. When Alaina returned, she told me the news that the
preconceptions of my interpretation surrounding my environment
were wiped clean. My mind was stimulated by numbers and forward
movement. I understand basic sociology and know people act in a
group how they normally would not act if by themselves. If power
and corruption enters, the picture, the entire ballgame, changes. I
would be chewed up and spit out. Multiple people with decades of
experience claim the same thing to authoritative figures against my
word. Who would be believed? I knew what was likely happening
but did not have enough circumstantial evidence to act on it. I would
continue my path forward as I had been doing.

I asked other clerks about what they thought about Alaina failing window training, and the echoed response was "language barrier."
I looked at our newly arrived T-7 Louise with utter apprehension.

The following day, Robin started at Newark. An intelligent PSE
with a lot of window experience. Robin was a hard worker, but more
important, she was honest.

Ted called me over. "Joel, you are going to window training next
week. It will be two weeks long."

The news was exciting but the dawn of a new challenge. I saw
the chess pieces set up in a larger game. What happened to Alaina
was awful. If I had a setback, it would be because my performance
warranted it and for no other reason. If I made regular, then that

would free my ability to help Jay gain control of his post office, and the supervisors would have a platform they could freely focus on developing themselves. I did not want to let the USPS down; I did not want to let Jay down.

That following morning after the scans were completed, Jay approached. "You're not working on July 4. I'm having Tim do it. I got to make sure you get a day off before you go to window school."

"Can I contact the instructor and get a copy of the book?"

"You're going to want to get hold of Candy in Columbus. She is the person to talk to."

I called. "Hi, Candy. My name is Joel Benner. I'm calling to see if there is any way I can get a copy of the Sales and Service Associate training book, I just really want to make sure I do well and hope to utilize the next couple of days to get a leg up on the material. All right, thank you. Oh! My number is 740-348-1234. Have a good day."

I hung up the phone.

Friday, July 5, 2019, the parcel volume following a holiday was always heavy. Alaina appeared forlorn, but I could tell she was keeping a positive attitude. Once the scans were completed, I was called in the back office. AJ sat at the supervisor's desk with a couple of sheets of paperwork. It was a predisciplinary interview for attendance. I had been late two times, but it was weeks ago and during split shifts and being called in, etc. It was especially confusing because I had never seen the supervisors show any authority or concern about the accountability of clerk's actions. I had been their greatest ally in impossible circumstances. I did not expect to receive special treatment—that is not what I'm saying—it just was out of the blue.

The entire thing was outlandish. After the PDI, I saw Jay near the PASS machine. He had directions to Twin Rivers postal headquarters. It was a huge mailing facility. It was where the area to POOM (post office operations manager) and OIG (office of inspector general) were located.

Jay said, "This is where you're going Monday."

"Am I going to pass?"

"I don't know, are you?"

"I don't know, am I?"

The day ended, and I tried to call AJ., but his phone went to voicemail. I talked to Ted.

Ted said, "Really, the only reason we did that was because we had to write Thelma up for calling off. We knew she would say it wasn't fair that we didn't write you and Alaina up." Alaina had a PDI for the delay a few weeks prior for being tardy on Amazon Sunday.

CHAPTER 5

Sales and Service Associate Academy

The following Monday, I woke up with laser focus. *I will not fail; I will pass. No one will take this from me. I will spend every waking hour studying. Failing will be an impossibility.* Every sense of my prefrontal cortex was ignited. My hippocampus was a dry sponge, ready to soak the vastness of information. My frontal lobes were alert and prepared. I arrived at Twin Rivers forty-five minutes early. I sat in my car, wishing I had the book. I wanted the book so badly. What I would not do for the book. Twenty minutes until the start time, I began my approach inside. I could feel my heart beating. A car could have wrecked behind me and I would not have noticed. The world was silent; there was only accomplishing what I was here to do. Pass this class and solidify my career with clean hands. "An honest man's pillow is his peace of mind."

The instructions read to wait by the elevators, and someone would guide the class up to the classroom. We exited outside and walked to the loading dock. Beside the giant doors was an entry. A multidecade veteran of the post office stood behind a counter. The guide introduced him, and he said comments about the USPS; although they weren't flattering, they were humorous and came from a good place. We continued through a plastic door, kind of like the long clothes you would see at a carwash, but this was plastic.

Through the plastic doors was a large workroom floor. We immediately turned to our right, and through another door entered a stairwell. We climbed six flights of stairs and entered another massive workroom floor. It was deserted, filled with pallets of empty mail bins. After a seventy-meter walk, there was a carpeted room, with five rows of tables and computer chairs, which would be fantastic to suffice my inability to sit still. A middle-aged woman, who seemed very articulate, greeted us one by one. "Good morning, good morning, good morning." She was nicely dressed. She was wearing a lot of jewelry, which is traditionally a sign of femininity, social status, and professionalism.

I entered the first row, walked to the end, left one chair open to my right, and placed my backpack on it. I removed two energy drinks, placing them to my right, leaving plenty of space for writing material and paper. Behind my drinks were my phone and my can of Grizzly wintergreen. After the stragglers joined the class, we began.

Michelle said, "Good morning. Welcome to the Sales and Service Associate Academy. My name is Michelle, and this is Miss Susan. (Miss Susan had a positive energy about her I found comforting. She was African American, in her late fifties or early sixties, and her speech suggested an upbringing rooted in the tenets of African Baptist Church, although that is merely an educated guess.) These are your books. They are to stay here. A few cycles ago, we had a student file a grievance because she wanted compensation for her study time. Do not worry. We will give you plenty of time to review."

Michelle gave all the formalities you would expect at a group orientation. We went around one by one, saying the one interesting fact about ourselves and our hobbies. After we all spoke, Michelle took her turn. She said her hobbies were traveling. Michelle was fluent in French. Looking her up on social media revealed she also had an interest in motorcycles. After an hour, we began the curriculum. The way the class was taught was interactive, so we all took turns reading a page. I followed along until the first fifteen-minute break. I found it difficult to read that slow and drifted. Once everybody had disbursed for the bathroom or to stretch their legs, I move forward in the literature, taking notes, etc. Premier products, market dominate, periodicals, the Postal Mission, the Postal Vision, what roles postmasters had within an organization, supervisors' scope of responsibility, etc. Everyone returned from break, and the class continued. When it was my turn to read, I flipped back several pages, read, and continued. The class was let out at 4:00 p.m. I closed the book but hated stopping. I asked Michelle and Miss Susan if I could please take the book with me. They denied my request. Walking out, I felt anxious. I needed that book. I wanted nothing more in my life. I had trouble sleeping that night.

The following morning, I arrived thirty minutes early, hoping to get an early jump on the reading. Michelle was there along with one other individual. I set up my desk—two energy drinks, my cell phone, and a can of grizzly wintergreen. I continued classes of mail, priority mail, balloon dimensioning, retail ground, six to eight days, maximum weight seventy pounds. Fir—

"Good morning, class," Michelle's voice broke my hypnotic state of formulating and processing new information.

"I hope everyone had a good night last night. I hope you all went home and didn't think about the post office. All right, I want everyone to stand up! Repeat after me: *Does this item contain anything liquid, fragile, perishable, or potentially hazardous such as lithium batteries or perfume?* Good! Sit down. All right, so questions over anything we covered?"

I raised my hand.

"Yes. Joel?"

"I have a question about the test. For the people who failed last class, was it because they missed too many questions or—"

Michelle was somewhat taken back but did not show any obvious signs of it. "Um, it's a Pass or Fail. It doesn't give us the test scores…"

"I guess I don't understand the three who failed the last cycle. Did they show signs that they were confused? Did they not listen?"

Miss Susan said, "Oh yeah, one girl even told us that they were making her come to this class and she didn't want to be on the window."

I was very transparent about my skepticism surrounding the integrity of the class prior. We broke for lunch; I had been dieting and training until the day I started the Window Academy. I ate only junk food while I was there—cookies, fudge rounds, etc. The brain is nearly a quarter of our energy output. The class was twelve business days long. Ten classroom days, one prep day and test day.

Long term, these choices in nutrition would be detrimental to health and cognitive abilities. Still, in a short period, it would maximize my learning potential. Humans are species of survival; our bodies want to carry plenty of body fat. The brain runs off carbohydrates. When we lose weight through dieting, our body produces a chemical called glucagon, and its purpose is to pull body fat from our fat stores, convert it to ketones, and that acts as an energy source for the brain and body. By dramatically switching my nutrition, my blood would flood with glucose, producing a euphoric state. Essentially, I aimed to allow my mind to put all its potential and energy for this task. Although my logic here would undoubtedly be argued.

A few minutes before lunch was over, Michelle spoke. "I messaged Alaina, just to check on her mental status… We talked for a little bit, talked about you…"

I responded as I usually do, "Oh yeah? Good or bad?" However, it was meant to be rhetorical.

She said, "It wasn't bad…"

I asked more questions about Alaina. "I am confused because she is a smart girl. I am unable to see the factor that caused her failure."

"She is smart," said Michelle. "Um, I don't think she's quite as studious as you are…"

The class continued, and I noticed Michelle's eyes glazed. This can occur for a multitude of reasons. Drugs use or stress response to a threat. Adrenaline causes the muscles around the eyes to constrict, leaving them sore or sensitive to light. I asked again if I could please take the book.

Miss Susan said, "Don't worry! You will be fine… Go home and relax!"

I drove home but could not relax. They allowed us to take our notes home, but that was it. I rewrote the notes I had taken into a 220-page binder, making them more organized with better penmanship.

Wednesday, I arrived and headed up to the classroom. It was locked this time. One other student was waiting. Michelle and Miss Susan arrived to let us in, and I sat in my spot. Two energy drinks, my cell phone, and a can of Grizzly Wintergreen. That day, Miss Susan taught the class, and Michelle sat and observed. That day we discussed the mailability of first-class letters. Ms. Susan asked, "What is the minimum length for a letter to be considered machinable?"

I raised my hand; she called my name. "The minimum and maximum length for a first-class letter to be considered machinable are between 5.5 and—"

"I ain't trying to hear all that!" said Miss Susan.

Someone else raised their hand and answered, "Five and a half inches." I knew that I needed to dial back my intensity.

After class, that Wednesday, I drove back to Newark and stopped by the post office. I wanted to see if Lance had his book if I could borrow it for two weeks. The rules were no textbooks were allowed outside of the classroom. The decision to break those rules was based on the lack of information about the failures of the cycle before me. There are thousands of ways someone could formulate questions in a test based on the eleven-module textbook. If the decision to prevent an individual were mitigated by hidden agendas, then the most likely course of success would be to familiarize myself to the extent possible with the material, making a failing score an impossible outcome. If I took the test and knew with complete certainty I did well, then I could argue the case; however, if there were gaps in my knowledge, then I had to accept the outcome. I needed job security. I accepted the risk.

I arrived at Newark, and I saw Luke and Bernie at the dispatch desk. I approached Bernie and said under my breath, "Hey, man, do you have your old book?"

"Yes, I'll bring it in to you tomorrow," said Bernie.

Life is complicated. People are victims of chance, and often the wicked reign victorious. I ask, am I in fact a fool for looking to do what is morally right instead of looking to do what is best for me in an environment? If I adopt that line of thinking, I would likely suffer far less anguish, with a higher probability of life success.

We try to raise our children to be good people. We might even take them to church and teach them about Christ dying on the cross, bearing the sins of humanity, yet we throw them out into the world and expect perseverance. Wolves are everywhere. Should I teach him to be deceitful and exploit when possible? Looking at success on the stage of life from a percentage outcome, that would be the smartest thing to do. I simply would not. I will teach my son to hold on to his values and defend himself from the wicked that walk the earth. There is one way and one way. In *The Power of Literature*, Dr. Jordan Peterson said something to a reporter that resonated with me in the most important time. "Why do people need to read?" Dr. Peterson said.

"Because you need great literature to live without undue suffering."

As class ended Friday, Michelle addressed the class and said, "All right, everyone, I want you to go home and not think about the post office, relax, spend time with your family, play with your kids, enjoy your time away from here." I packed up my things and made my way to the parking lot and drove to the Newark Post Office. Bernie saw me, and we walked out to his little green Chevy S-10. I watched him pull out this slightly used SSA book.

The feelings I felt were indescribable—so much relief. Bernie had just saved my life. I wasted no time. I drove to Walmart and bought four packages of flash cards. It was 7:00 p.m. and I knew every second was critical. Every second I could squeeze in might be the difference between a pass or fail. I read, "PS Form 3800 provides the sender with a barcode receipt..."

I took out a flash card and wrote, "What does PS Form 3800 do?"

I provided the answer on the back. I read in my car and continued to construct more flashcards. Saturday around noon, I completed the textbook. I turned to page 1 and started from the beginning.

Monday morning, I arrived in Twin Rivers and made my way up to the classroom. Michelle greeted the class. "Good morning! I hope everyone had a good weekend. All right! I want you to look at your neighbor. I want you to spend the next few minutes getting to know them. Go!"

The next few days were a blur of fact memorization, reading, and flashcard making. I had over four hundred flashcards.

Leaving Twin Rivers, my first stop was at Lady Jane's haircuts for guys, I made an appointment with my hairstylist of two years. Her name was Kaitlyn Blevins.

I said, "Kaitlyn, I want you to give me the best haircut you have ever given. This is the most important haircut I will ever receive. Can you do that?"

Kaitlyn said, "I always do."

I explained to her the magnitude of importance the following day was for me and although all her haircuts were excellent, this one was a step above. I left a large gratuity and thanked her for her time. Next was the hobby lobby where I purchased two small gifts, one for Miss Susan and one for Michelle. My next stop was at Kohl's. I purchased brand-new clothing along with a watch. I received a men's window clerk dress shirt from a gentleman who recently retired and left behind. I ironed it, laid out all my apparel for the following day, and went to bed.

The following day, I woke up, jumped out of bed, and hopped in the shower. I allowed myself plenty of time to arrive on time if ran into traffic. I pulled into the parking lot, found a space, put the car into park, and shut off the engine. I exhaled deeply.

"Okay, Joel, this is it. You got this. You got this, you got this." I opened the door, walking tall and confident. Entering the building, the first person I saw was a young lady scrolling on her phone, we made eye contact, and she snapped up straight like maybe I was some-one important. I continued through the plastic sleeve door, opened the stairwell door, and up the stairs I went. Everyone that day looked phenomenal. We were all ready to do this! Michelle looked stressed. I saw Miss Susan, and when she saw me, she turned the other way. She came back after a few minutes and said, "I'm scared of you!"

I brought the two gifts with me, and my choices were:

1. wait until after the test completed.
2. Give the gifts to them before the test.

I made a judgment call based on their body language to give it to them before. I presented the gifts to both Michelle and Ms. Susan. Miss Susan covered her mouth and looked up. "Thank you, Lord! Thank you, Lord! Thank you, Lord!"

"Oh my gosh, Joel! Thank you so much—it means so much to us."

I will never know, but maybe that was the wisest choice I ever made to date as a postal employee. Candy was the person administrating the test. They had us line up by the door, and I anxiously awaited while they called us in one by one. It was one hundred multiple-choice questions. When it came to my turn, I followed the instructions given and waited. My computer did not respond. I had to start over reentering all the information and wait again for it to load. After ten minutes, they had me switch to another computer and reenter my information. Another ten minutes passed by, and at this point, the test had been going on for thirty-five minutes. People began finishing. A few seconds later, the wording prompted to click the button to begin the test.

1. The responsibility of the SSA is to offer what?
   A. Products
   B. Customer service
   C. Assistance with packaging
   D. Solutions

I finished in fifteen minutes but was the last one to complete it. Did I know with certainty I passed? No, I didn't and could not argue a failing outcome. Michelle and Miss Susan walked in, and Michelle sat down with a disappointed look on her face. My knees shook, and I knew it was a done deal.

Miss Susan grabbed the paper. "How you going to score that, child! *You passed!*"

CHAPTER 6

Checks and Balances

"Passed!" I said.

"*Awesome!*" said Jay. "Congratulations and thank you!"

"I gave it all I had, left nothing back. Thank you for the opportunity. Tomorrow four a.m.?"

"Yes, four a.m."

"Sounds good."

"See you then."

July 17, 2019, I was back in the office. I wondered how things had changed and what was going on. The postal service was the same task every day. When anomalies occurred, the pattern broke. It could be people's moods, a decrease in volume followed by a spike in volume. One sales and service rep would call off, upsetting another SSA, and then she would call off to make things fair. The environment could never maintain stability for more than a few days. When I say stability, I mean the group of employees performing job duties per employment agreement and going home. It was always being manipulated. It made it impossible to habituate and was extremely stressful. I do not have the ability to neglect or ignore things that needed to be performed if it was in my ability to do them. The pursuit of the knowledge in this book is a byproduct of my attempts to be in a stable environment—find the problems causing grief and resolve them.

Nothing stood out at me right away. Alaina saw me, and I gave her a friendly, good morning. We worked and sorted parcels. The first hour, things were fine, and she received a text message. I could tell someone messaged her informing her I passed window training. Her preconceptions I would fail were probably right. It just didn't happen. The explanation could be anyone's guess. Alaina stopped working and watched videos on her phone. I sympathized with her feelings and the unfairness she had received. I wish there were something I could have done, but it was the only thing I could do.

Thelma had moved to a 6:00 a.m. spot. After we completed parcel scans, we spread the DPS letter trays. Once the city-side DPS letters were staged for carrier pickup, Sam, Thelma, Alaina, and I worked our way to the rural route side. Thelma and Sam shoved the cart of DPS toward Alaina and walked away. Sam said "Come on" and beckoned me to follow them. I was appalled. Thelma was the new gun for hire in the morning.

I looked at Alaina's face and she had a blank stare as if this were her reality and she had to accept it. I thought in my head, *Not while I'm breathing!* I went over, helped Alaina, and we finished the DPS. Aliana was as surprised to see me assisting as I was that she was surprised. That type of abysmal behavior isn't common within civilized people. It is found within groups of sociopaths. Prisons and gains would be a prime example of a group of people gaining hierarchy by inflicting pain on the weak. I had been on the receiving end for months but could never connect it as tactical until I witnessed it from a bystander's point of view. Thelma was instructed to do that. Her reaction to me helping Alaina was, "Awww, Joel is so nice. See, Sam?"

A legitimate endearing response to something egregious she had initiated. It was as if I gained a hitman's respect for jumping out in front of a bullet to save a target. That is exactly what Alaina was. A new target, a business move. To imagine Thelma would do that without some type of incentive wasn't possible; there wasn't any emotion behind it. It was just business.

Alaina blushed. "You…you are different. You are not the same."

I didn't respond. The biggest sources of insight to corruption are when people attempt to hurt other people. It has driven my understanding and aided in my desire to stop it. Not because I want to be a hero, a saint, or a paladin but because it is unnecessary, ignorant, and barbaric. Power and respect should be earned with morality and contribution according to the environment people are in. People sell drugs on the street; respect and power are earned according to that environment. When that evil behavior enters a professional establishment is when further investigation is warranted. To ignore it would be at my own peril.

At 11:00 a.m. that day, I was standing over towards the dispatch desk. Jay walked in. It was the first time I had seen him since I left for window training. He shook my hand and congratulated me. Engaged in small talk, Jay was telling me about the postal museums, and back in colonial ages, people called the postmaster "Your Honor." Jay looked at me and said, "You know, you remind me of my son."

At that moment, something happened, which was the opening of Pandora's box. Thelma screamed from the other side of the cases, "Oh! Is that Jay? *I know how to handle him!*" She came speed walking over to us, looked at him with the wrath of God in her eyes, and said, "*Don't you even!*" and stormed off.

It was another puzzle piece. If I could not make it fit now, it would only be a matter of time. To see a clerk speak to a postmaster that way was absurd. It would be the equivalency of giving a judge the middle finger before sentencing. Such disrespect and public insult can be suggestive only this individual felt comfortable doing it. But why? Even the Union could not defend against such actions. My radar had continued to be narrowed. The first thing I felt I had to do was to remove myself from the tension if somehow, I was involved.

I texted Jay, "Hey, Jay, I just want you to know. My mind stimulates by numbers and performance, so you will never have to worry about me acting in accordance with an individual or individual's emotions. Contributing to a business I believe in is what makes me happy and fulfilled. So if you're on the side of success, profit revenue, and consumer satisfaction, then you can guarantee I'm right with you. I am ignorant of any personal issues between employees, so if you see me like someone's picture or something, it's just because I am polite. I am just not wired to be like that. I just want to learn and grow as much as I can in Newark and progress from there. The Newark Post Office will be the Mecca of performance! Like you can go through my phone lol."

Jay replied, "It's all good. I have no problems with you. Thanks for letting me know, though. You might be regular this Saturday."

I felt better after reading Jay's text, but still, it was so strange. What could it have been about? A USPS clerk required a set number of hours of window time before they were qualified to become a full-time employee. I trained with Thelma and Louise.

"Hi, Joel! Today you are just going to watch," said Louise.

I had my blank flash cards, ready to take notes. It was so exciting.

Thelma said, "It's been a while since we had some eye candy up here!"

There is a passage in Proverbs I'll never forget:

> For the lips of an immoral woman are as sweet as
> honey, and her mouth is smoother than oil. But
> in the end, she is as bitter as poison, as dangerous
> as a double edge sword. (Proverbs 5:3–4)

I smiled; it's a difficult situation because you have to be friendly to an extent. Whenever I encountered a compliment or sexual gesture, whether that was one female saying I was handsome, etc., I was careful not to verbally respond with other than "thank you."

Thelma intrigued me in many ways; I just had never met someone with her personality. It was not an evil personality. She was a wise woman in her early forties that adopted behaviors that had been taught or learned by working twenty years in the postal service. She understood me to an extent. She knew what I liked to hear, what she could say to guide my thinking that no one else would pick up on. The only time I saw legitimate anger from Thelma was surrounding an issue discussed later. Everything else was simply business.

Having felt Thelma's complimentary words were likely for the purpose of creating conflict, I began observing reactions of males amongst the workroom floor. Louise was different. I think she legitimately found me attractive, which is a large reason why I became regular if I am allowed to be blunt. Jay assumed my work ethic was because I was loyal to him. He misinterpreted my personality. I am loyal to my employers because they provide me with advancement opportunity. It just so happened Jay's goals coincided with mine because he wanted the postmaster's position at Newark. That was as far as his vision extended. He saw me as a machine that defended against those who interfered with his goals.

I was impressionable because the reality of what was happening isn't something that I would put in the mix of possibilities. I think the depth of one's scope is reflective of the speed at which his or her understanding unfolds. I understand the consequences of personal action, with a belief system that is accepting toward forward movement would be a lag in identifying actions that are dubious in nature. Here is an example.

Imagine if I hired ten people to build a car, and they did. Everything was perfect, all nuts and bolts were fastened according to the spec sheet, etc. I go to start it. Nothing. After weeks of troubleshooting and retracing steps, you identify where the problem occurred. What do you think it was?

Answers: One of the mechanics put the garden hose in the gas tank, filling it up with water because he thought it was the gas pump.

Our thoughts filter the way we see the world. It took me months to find the water in the gas tank because I didn't even consider it a possibility because it carries such ignorance and damning consequences. Jay interpreted me as someone he could control for his own gain.

Window training continued, and after the first day of training, Louise allowed me on her unit while she monitored my actions. The first customer came in. It was an individual mailing a priority package. Louise instructed me. "Okay, now hit Mailing/Shipping."

I felt her body touch mine and I jumped. Louise said startlingly, "I'm sorry, I didn't mean to press myself against you."

I legitimately jumped because of the unexpected contact. Her reaction indicated offense and premeditation. I said awkwardly, "Oh, that's okay."

A couple of days later, while on the window, Thelma commented, "Joel, you're a rule follower, aren't you?"

My unfiltered response was, "Well, I think if one is thinking in the sense of long term, then that would be the wisest choice."

I completed on-the-job training, and I was awarded full-time status. It was a huge accomplishment, and I was proud to be a part of a 230-year-old organization that delivered 47 percent of the world's mail.

CHAPTER 7

Insight and a Knowledge Explosion

In early August 2019, I began my contractual position as the sales and service dispatch associate. My hours were 10:00 a.m. to 7:00 p.m. I arrived at work two hours early every day and did Hero training courses online. I completed forty classes. The USPS had only about ten with anything to do with the postal service, the rest of the educational material surrounding business ethics, personal development for supervisors, etc. The Hero website has much to offer the postal employees as far as education and information is concerned.

We had two new clerks start their employment at the Newark Post Office. I watched closely to ensure their experience was nothing like mine. The utter importance of hiring and retaining quality employees was paramount. I knew that interfering and stopping any abuse or hazing behaviors would cause a momentum toward excellence. An inherent right those who started employment before me had not received, which is undoubtedly the reason behind the swinging door of employees that had arrived before me. Not very many people are willing to indulge in behaviors that I witnessed with Alaina. Throughout the decades and the millions of people who came and gone into the USPS the Postal Reorganization Act of 1970 provided an arena for certain personalities to grow and manifest within the organization.

When a facility reaches stable operations, its increasingly easier to identify the bullet holes, where the bleeding is coming from. I was premature in my knowledge and understanding of postal operations and needed to understand. I ordered an Epson Ink tank printer. I now had the ability to print out thousands of pages of documents without replacing the ink. When the ink ran out, it was as simple as a nine-dollar purchase on Amazon and refilling the tank with a squeeze bottle preloaded with ink.

To understand an organizations current state, I had to know the history. I feel many financially Savvy people come into the picture and try to fix this large business with a calculator and pencil. On paper, it looks fantastic. There is no plausible reason it should not work. Why doesn't it?

I ordered several books online, one of which was *How the Post Office Created America* by Winifred Gallagher. I started from the beginning.

CHAPTER 8

Postal Circus

Early September of 2019, an event happened, which someone can look at in two ways. The first way is, I brought an immeasurable amount of trouble on myself by speaking freely to the wrong person, or the second way, by speaking freely, a chain of events unfolded that forced me to adapt and gain the necessary knowledge that would serve as an aid in making the USPS a stronger entity. I guess time will tell.

On September 8, 2019, I was looking on social media and came across a post by Thelma. It concerned locals and drug use. I approached her and said her post make her look crazy.

"I'm not crazy. You're crazy!" That comment ignited a war within the Newark Post Office I desperately wanted to be over with. The following morning at 10:00 a.m., I walked into the dispatch area obliterated. There were empty parcel bags on top of the dispatch desk. I approached the supervisors with this issue hoping mediation could take place.

On September 10, the same thing happened again. The dispatch area was destroyed, and empty parcel bags were placed on my desk. I went to Jay, expecting to have his support because I still had hope we were a team, and together, we were making the Newark Post Office the example of what excellence could be.

Jay told me, "Don't worry. I'll take care of it." He walked out on the floor and removed the empty parcel bag off my desk, but no mediation was attempted.

I could not wrap my head around it. Other clerks began giving me terrible looks. The carriers acted if a circus sideshow was occurring right in front of their eyes. It was entertainment.

September 11, the same thing happened again. One thing I know for certain was people will do morally wrong things until the consequences of that action affected them personally. They acted in accordance to suffice their own needs regardless of who was impacted. I saw the bags and thought to myself, *Well, I'll try something new.*

I approached Tim. "*Who put those bags on my desk?*"

A deer-in-headlights look appeared on Tim.

Tim said, "I don't know…"

I walked over to Sid. "*Who put those bags on my desk!*"

Sid gave the same response. I walked over to Bernie. "*Why is it every morning I walk in, there are bags on my desk?*"

At first, Bernie was taken back but did not want to appear weak, so he elevated his voice. Bernie said, "Wasn't me!"

"Calm down, bro!" said Sam.

"Oh, you want me to calm down?"

I walked outside and moved FSS carts onto the truck, and our maintenance man, James, approached me.

James said, "Remember what I told you? You're the low man on the totem pole, once you've been here for a year, things will get better, but you can't act that way because they all are going to say you are crazy!"

I needed to hear that. I genuinely apologized to everyone I shouted at and shook their hand. Sam would not shake my hand, but I understood.

On September 16, I walked into work, and there the bags were. I walked to my desk and placed my book on top of the bags then read the Employee Labor Manual. There were people staged anxiously waiting to witness an event. I had two questions.

1. Why do they not want me at the Newark Post Office?
2. Why didn't management attempt mediation?

I was consistent in my work ethic and mood; I was kind to everyone. I did not gossip. I always acknowledged people for their performance on both sides of a coin; that should be a positive factor in any work environment. What about Thelma prevented Jay from talking to her and mediating the situation? Why didn't the supervisors ever perform group talks?

September 19, I entered the Newark Post Office at my usual time. I always saw Tim first. He said, "Joel, Joel! The dancing machine." I think it was a term referring to a monkey, but I always found it funny.

I replied, "Good morning, Tim."

Tim said, "Hey, Thelma, thinks you took her bang energy drink. She said 'That's okay, I'll get him back.'"

"Well, I have to report it. It is a hearsay threat."

I approached AJ and repeated what Tim had told me.

AJ said, "*You clerks are the neediest people!*"

AJ's response was troublesome. It was suggestive that he encouraged the employees to take matters into their own hands. The contention could have been resolved with simple mediation. Why was it allowed to go on?

I asked, "Will you talk to her?"

AJ replied, "Well, I guess I have to, huh?"

An hour later, AJ informed me that Thelma said that she's scared of me, and she e-mailed all of her family saying, "*If I am murdered at work, it's because Joel Benner killed me.*"

My reply was "Okay." The most important thing I could do is keep com.

It is a scary thing when you find yourself in bizarre situations. I asked myself, *How did I get here?* I received a credible job, with a respectable salary, and end up in a conflict that feels more like a psychological study over human interaction in halfway houses? More so, how do I explain this to my family? Who would believe it? Honestly…who?

If someone told me they are experiencing what I am experiencing, I would not believe it the tales. It is that unbelievable. I knew right then I would have to write down everything that happened with dates, times, and pictures. The truth was I applied to work a government job that upholds truth and integrity. I joined a historic organization that takes pride in their services and strives to be competitive in the marketplace. I did not volunteer for a circus.

The big question then, "What do I do?" I begin by asking myself, *Am I right?* Take away the personal bias. Look at me from a third-person viewpoint and ask, "Are you justified or not?" The ability to hold yourself accountable dramatically impacts experience moving forward. I had to be overly critical of my actions and the words that came out of my mouth. I could not afford to let my guard down. Doing so would tie the knot in which I would hang.

Dispatch area upon arrival.

I could have contacted the Union but wanted to use the postal hierarchy to see if the situation could be resolved. Jay had not yet been granted the postmaster position, and his primary focus was landing the permanent postmaster position in Newark, Ohio.

With such little interference in an escalated situation, I could reasonably assume that he did not have control of his post office. The biggest question, again was, "Why?"

CHAPTER 9

Uncharted Territory

"Just give me two more weeks and I'll take care of it. Soon as I'm postmaster."

I talked to Jay for about fifteen minutes. I felt this woman was on a warpath. Slander, destruction, something about me soured her, and it went deeper than a rude comment. At first, it was distance, then unity, now its aggression. She was good at it, as if she has done it before. Thelma was vicious. I made a judgment call and considered two possibilities.

Thelma had some type of blackmail over Jay.

Jay was instructing Thelma to do it.

There absolutely could not be any other possibility. It was obviously destructive to the environment, for a man whose sole responsibility was ensuring successful operations of a post office; putting an end to the insanity should have been an action that required no thought.

Jay had been at the office all day. The parcels were dispatched, and I was about to do my end-of-day scans. I saw the postmaster prepare to leave the building. I approached him one last time to see if there could be a means to an end. It was thirty minutes of pacifying with Luke manically agreeing with Jay.

"I am a man of integrity and I do not want to be caught in a 'It's going to be me or you' situation," I said.

Jay replied, "I'll take care of it." He looked at Luke. "We gotta start doing things right from now on."

Jay left, but it didn't satisfy me. They were pacifying, arbitrary words that carried no meaning or intent behind them.

I could wait no longer. I had to take matters into my own hands. The union was my absolute last resort. On September 24, 2019, I emailed the post office operations manager (POOM), Jay's boss, explaining his attention was required. Bradley Grubb was the Area 2 post office operations manager. His job was to oversee post offices within Area 2 of the Ohio Valley District.

I walked over to the computer. Luke had shut the lights off. I could tell he was nervous, "Uh...Joel? It's time to go, okay?"

I replied, "I can't, Luke."

He stood there a few more seconds. "Oh, okay then, I'm off to the campground."

The door shut behind Luke, and the e-mail screen appeared. I explained to the POOM I believed things were happening in the background, and I was a man of integrity, that I would not sacrifice my moral compass.

Send. I logged out of the computer; my phone dinged.

Text message from Jay: "Are you still at the office?"

I replied, "Yes."

My phone rang. I knew this was it.

"Did you message the POOM?"

"Yes, sir. I did."

"Did I not tell you I would take care of it?"

"Jay, it's...not...like..."

"Even after I talked to you for thirty minutes!"

" ... "

"Do you want a transfer?"

"No, sir."

"Tomorrow, you and I will talk."

The following morning, I entered the Newark Post Office. I saw Postmaster Jay. He instructed me to check my e-mail, that the POOM sent me something. I logged into my e-mail account. It read, "Joel, call me. (614) 788-1234."

I walked outside to gain privacy and dialed the number.

"Hello, Joel?"

"Yes, sir.

"I got your e-mail, is someone doing something illegal?"

"It's more complicated than that, sir. I can't say—I have no proof."

"What do you mean? Hello? Joel?"

"Sir, I don't feel comfortable talking here. I made an observation report—can I send it to you?"

"Yes, I want to see it."

I hung up the phone with Grubb and walked back to the office. At lunchtime, I e-mailed him the observation report I had made last night after I left.

1. Unprofessional relationship between the lead sales service associate and the postmaster.
    *   Informal and unprofessional conduct. IE. Coming and going as the individual pleases into the postmaster's quarters, public and open sexual innuendos. "I see you, boo boo."
2. The daily smell of alcohol protruding from the lead sales service associate following her lunch break.
    *   Attention toward this concern was not investigated.
3. Hostile/tension-filled, interaction between the postmaster and clerk who filled the previously vacant LSSA position.
    *   Twice I witnessed an emotional outburst from the previously acting LSSA clerk directed toward the postmaster. The first occurrence was early July, following the postmaster's vacation to West Virginia. I would describe this individual's anger stemming from betrayal: "Oh, don't you even!"
    *   The next occurrence happened roughly thirty days later, early to mid-August, where the previously acting LSSA clerk had an outburst, shouting, "All men are dicks." The outburst was directed toward the postmaster. More details on these occasions if requested.

4. Complete and utter lack of insight from supervisors pertaining to postal operations within the facility.
   - Absence of planning. Avoidable problems are handled as they happen and unprofessionally. IE pivots being thrown on the backs of unsuspecting carriers. "Go do this."
   - Absence of problem-solving.
   - Absence of communication between supervisors and bargaining position employees. All performance-related issues have failed to be transferred. It never makes it to the low-level employees.
   - Apprehension dealing with customer-related issues. It is difficult getting them to come and address issues at the front window that requires a supervisor's attention.
   - The conflict between each other.
   - Apprehension in dealing with conflict resolution.

   I approached the supervisor with an issue pertaining to a "hearsay threat." A fellow clerk had informed me of another clerk's intention to seek revenge for an energy drink beverage disappearing in the break room refrigerator. I took this issue to one so the situation could be resolved by ensuring the accusing clerk I did not take her beverage and no retaliation toward myself would be necessary. The Supervisors response was, "You clerks are the neediest people!" The remark was heard by multiple people. The remark was unprofessional and validated taking matters into one's own hands is appropriate.

5. Complete and utter lack of structure and business ethics
   - Absence of performance evaluations
   - Absence of feedback about employee performance
   - Absence of group goals, i.e., what we are doing well, what we can improve on

6. Euphoric and sudden mood changes surrounding the supervisors following the end of day 1412 and after I sign for the 3854-registry dispatch book.
   - Upbeat mood.

- Nightly questioning by the supervisor. My responses are relayed back via group text.
- Both closing supervisors have made remarks seeking insurance of my state of mind, questions that are vague and peculiar. "Can I trust you? "Do you make more than me?" etc.

7.   Panic and negotiating when I informed the supervisor of my decision to contact the AREA 2 POOM regarding my concerns of the integrity of postal operations.

This was uncharted territory for me. we hear stories of government workers who are reporting wrongdoing all the time, and it hardly ever ends up good for them. I continued the day with a heavy heart. I destroyed myself to give this man a platform. He gave me a great job, and I wanted to ensure he received the postmaster's position. He misinterpreted my personality.

Later that day, Jay called me in the office to talk one on one. "I told you I would take care of it! How are you going to message my boss?"

I told Jay it was a gut feeling, but honestly, I believed it was more spiritual. Jay told me I had stabbed him in the back, and I hated he felt that way because I respected Jay so much. What he did not acknowledge was a mutual respect sprouts from honesty in intent. We worked for the same organization, and as a subordinate, my job was to obey all lawful orders with the notion those orders coincided with the entity that employs us. I believed my efforts contributed to crime. I was the one who was stabbed in the back.

CHAPTER 10

Never-Ending Documenting

An important factor many people fail to see is the repetitiveness of the job. It is the same thing every day. That is not a bad thing necessarily. It allows me to learn other hobbies. I'm able to focus my cognitive energy in new or interesting topics. Here is a good example.

Many people listen to audiobooks while driving to work. Well, one might say, "How can you listen to a book and drive?" Because you drive every day.

With that in mind, anytime something happened, it broke the pattern of repetitiveness, like a box fan being turned off and back on again. As a post office becomes more efficient, it is easier to pinpoint phenomena. The stories of insanity in a postal unit likely occur to disguise corruption.

Every time the pattern broke, it came from the same people. Management.

Following the short conversation I had with the POOM, my work area appeared as it should have. Nothing was ever permanent. Normalcy lasted a week. I had tried writing essays. I made an inspirational postal video that received thousands of views. I suggested to management group talks occur. Nothing worked. I wanted my peers to be happy so badly they just were not. I understand not everyone is self-content and the need for proper environment is prevalent in order to maintain a fulfilled staff. There must be some type of goals or challenges introduced to a group of people or else they would formulate their own.

I had turned into their entertainment. My actions were new. They were exciting. They were informative. It was a break from the monotony. It became so reoccurring that the ability to empathize dissipated. They saw it as a group goal and challenge. I knew it would not stop.

Thelma acted terrified when I entered the building in the morning. Whenever she would walk by me, I stood still and looked up at the ceiling. Now the aim was to attack my sanity. I wasn't a big conversationalist in the first place, but I was being bated into saying something they could use. It all went back to checks and balances.

This continued for six days, on October 8, 2019. I had posted a positive post on the Newark Post Office social media page, and Thelma made a laughing emoji underneath. I wanted only peace and success for our post office, and we were on our way there. Anytime anything happened, I had to address it in the most appropriate fashion. I issued a written document.

LETTER OF WARNING
NEWARK OHIO MANAGEMENT STAFF
EMPLOYEE: Joel Benner
10/08/2019
EIN-12345678

This letter is my last attempt to resolve an ongoing issue on the grounds of *defamation of character*. On September 19, I approached a supervisor and informed him of a hearsay threat for retaliation involving a missing energy drink from the break room. The following day, I approached the same supervisor to inquire if the issue had been resolved. The supervisor informed me that the involving clerk had e-mailed all her family members, stating, "If I'm murdered at work, it's because Joel Benner killed me." Since the information given was in a formal setting by an appointed supervisor, it should be taken literally. Defamation of character is a false statement intending to cause damage to a person's reputation. The above incident is a defamatory statement: *a statement held up to scorn or ridicule of contempt by the right-thinking group of people.* In layman's terms, the people in which I work with management staff and peers. Since the incident, my mental state has been questioned multiple times. I always document any feedback about my performance, both good and bad—the most recent being last night, October 7, 2019, by the closing supervisor. I asked the closing supervisor if he was a psychologist. He informed me he was not. I then informed him that making assumptions regarding an employee's mental condition was a slippery slope. In my continued attempt to work in an environment free of harassment outlined in the Employee Labor Manual 673.4, any further claims or allegations made without adequate proof or credentials pertained to myself will be addressed in a *professional manner.* Any further claims involving the individual who made the statement will be addressed in a *legal manner.*

I handed the document to Ted. Ted was very smart, very literate. He looked at the document and guided me back to Jay's office. He handed the paper to Jay.

His reaction was surprising. "What is this? What's this all about?"

Ted pointed to certain areas on the paper for Jay to look at. Jay took a minute, and studied the paper more thoroughly.

"*That's it! I have had it!* I'm getting Jennifer (the Union president) here! I'm contacting the POOM!"

I felt a slight tingle of fear, and Jay caught it.

"Yes, we're going to get this settled."

Replaying the incident in my head over and over, I formulated my perception of what just happened. Literacy is huge in leadership. I cannot express the utter value reading and continued personal development has in effectiveness surrounding management.

> Functional illiteracy—reading and writing skills inadequate to manage daily living and employment tasks that requires reading skill beyond a basic level.

What was interesting was Jay picked up on my emotions and played them with no hesitation. He was brilliant at it. He wasn't extremely literate, though. I could see how Louise and Jay would be the perfect team. It would be a perfect partnership. The T-7 (Louise) falls under the protection of the Union and has impenetrable job security. Even if money were found missing, you would have to catch the individual with the hand in the cookie jar. I thought to myself, *Wait. It's not that simple.*

What I took from those two minutes was they had never picked up a postal manual in their lives. How in the world did they make it as far as they did? I would soon discover.

CHAPTER 11

Meeting with the POOM

Friday, October 15, 2019. I entered work at my start time of 10:00 a.m. I was on the window with Bernie. Bernie and I were friends. He was the second hardest worker at the Newark Post Office. (I would frequently tease him, but the truth is no one worked harder than Bernie.) He would always reply with "Boy, I'm fifty years old, I'll still run circles around you." Bernie and I helped customers, and it's nice being in good company. Customers sense when there is conflict. When individuals are together, working in unison is what produces amazing results. While Bernie and I assisted customers, Jay, Thelma, Tim, and Ted were in the back offices convening.

Twenty-five minutes later, Jay came and brought me back for questioning. Jay replied, "Okay, Joel, I have a couple of papers here that you wrote—why don't you tell me about them?" I cannot quote verbatim the entire meeting, but I will get close.

"Anytime an issue happens like this one…"

"Issue of what?"

"Defamation of character, a defamatory statement…"

"I do not need the definition—I know what *defamation* is."

I looked over Tim (our Union rep). He had a big notebook, scribbling something. I took this matter profoundly serious, but when I looked at Tim, he was wearing blue mesh shorts, ankle socks, an Ohio state shirt, and a generic ball cap that probably was older them me. Just a good old boy that has seen many years inside these walls. I smiled earnestly at Tim.

Jay continued, "Tell me what you mean by unprofessional." (He was referring to the observation report.) The T-7 comes and goes as she pleases?

"So it's called Integration by the Academics. It precludes accountability for wrongdoing."

"I have an open-door policy, Joel. You have gone in before."

"Yes, but I always knock. The postmaster quarters is a sacred place you can't just walk in."

"I have an open-door policy."

Tim stuck his finger in the air and wanted to say something, but the words would not come out of his mouth; he went back to scribbling on the note pad. I laughed.

After another ten minutes of banter, I said, "I just want to get along with my coworkers." And I looked at Thelma and said, "Okay, Thelma, can we please get along?" (I liked Thelma's West Virginian accent. It came out so pronounced at specific times. Primarily when she was at the window and she used her customer service voice, or when she was furious.)

Thelma said, "I don't talk about you I don't look at you. You make me uncomfortable ever since you wanted to show me pictures of your dick!"

"OK! This conversation is over."

It was so premeditated, looking back on the facial expressions of "horrific shock" that appeared on the management team's face.

Once the meeting was adjourned, Ted came up to me. "I wish you would have said that it wasn't true."

"I will not respond to dubious statements. If she wants to go that route, she must prove it's persistent and pervasive. Ted, all these people talk about is sex!"

He nodded in agreement. Ted and I walked to the docking area. "Look, Joel, I'm trying to get out of here, man. I'm looking for post-master positions near Columbus."

Jay handed me a paper and said, "You have a meeting with the POOM Monday morning."

M - Newark, OH

Subject: Joel Benner
Location: 850 Twin Rivers Drive Rm 210 Columbus, OH 43216

Start: Mon 10/21/2019 11:30 AM
End: Mon 10/21/2019 12:00 PM
Show Time As: Tentative

Recurrence: (none)

Meeting Status: Not yet responded

Organizer: Grubb, Bradley - Columbus, OH
Required Attendees: - Newark, OH

Importance: High

Good Morning **JAY**

Bradley is requesting an one on one meeting with Joel Benner and himself on Monday 10/21/2019 at 11:30 am in his office. Please confirm that Joel will be in attendance.

He can call my phone at 614. 10 upon arrival at the elevators downstairs in order to come up.

Thank you,

Karen J
USPS POOM 1,3 and 4 Secretary
850 Twin Rivers Dr. RM 210
Columbus, OH 43216-9992
Phone: 6
fax: 614. 2

A SMILE CAN MAKE A DIFFERENCE!!!

Over the weekend, I prepared a letter of address to the post office operations manager. I would analogize his rank as a full bird colonel. It was a big deal seeing him in person. Luke had mentioned he had not even met him before. I wrote the letter and rehearsed it until I felt confident. I could comfortably say it without jumbling my words. I got a fresh haircut and purchased black dress pants, a crisp white dress shirt perfectly pressed, and a black tie. My ID tag was pinned appropriately. Monday at 8:00 a.m., I stopped by the office with a folder full of supporting documentation. I approached Stacey recently back from maternity leave. She was the morning supervisor.

I asked Stacey if she had a copy of the e-mail with directions to Twin Rivers, but really, I wanted to watch people's reactions, primarily the morning clerks. One precursor to chaos is when an absence of leadership and business ethics leaves a group of people. It turns into a tribalistic atmosphere. When they saw me in formal clothing, it was like I witnessed them snapping out of a trance produced by the environment. I guess a better way of putting it is, it was an unknown occurrence that yielded self-preservation. Behaviors that were questionable or borderline paused until they knew the cause for concern had dissipated. I walked out and proceeded to my car and made the thirty-minute drive to Columbus.

I entered the Twin Rivers drive building and found the number to the POOM's office next to the elevator shaft. I dialed the extension. Grubbs's secretary answered the phone, "Bradley Grubbs's office, how may I help you?"

I replied, "Hi, I'm Joel Benner. I have a meeting today with the POOM." The secretary said she would be right down to get me.

A couple of minutes later, the elevator doors opened, and a woman guided me outside his office. "Have a seat right here. Mr. Grubb will be right out to get you."

A few seconds later, a man came. "Joel?"

I replied, "Yes, sir."

The POOM escorted me back to the office. We talked. The following conversation is close but not verbatim.

"All right! You look like an army guy. I am an army guy myself. Where were you stationed?"

"Fort Drum, New York, sir."

The POOM and I had a lot of things in common; we both were army veterans, air assault-certified, etc.

"Tell me about this Thelma. I heard her name before…"

"She's dangerous, sir. Um, I prepared a letter of address."

"Okay, I can look at it later."

"I would like to read it, sir, if that's okay."

Letter of Address to Area 2 POOM and Associates

On behalf of the Newark Post Office, I appreciate everyone taking time out of their busy schedules to address the issues I will cover over the next four minutes. I feel this will paint a clear picture of what is going on by using facts only. This will expedite a solution to problems at hand.

Our postal service is in a state of emergency. It was clarified in the meeting between Congress and Postmaster Brennen; even with the repeal of the mandated retirement fund, we are still losing billions a year. I feel this is relevant to the situation here because post offices nationwide operate under virtually the same procedures. There is only one workplace environmental attitude that will yield a surplus in profit revenue and only one environmental attitude that guarantees safety, teamwork, and overall well-being among the employees, and that is the desire to do a job effectively and proficiently to carry out the postal mission. Over the next few minutes, I will briefly take you through significant events beginning May 2, leading to this very moment.

Beginning employment at the Newark Post Office my initial thoughts were positive. Everyone was friendly and informative. The morning parcel scan was completed by 8:00 a.m. One week later, the conflicts began primarily with the lowest-ranking PSE in terms of seniority. (Alaina) relentlessly ordering, shouting, and control over what task I conducted. Any actions performed without her approval resulted in new task, equally important but at her delegation. My first payday at the Newark Post Office paychecks did not come. I was also missing an entire day from that paycheck.

On June 1 [The POOM took notes], the Newark Post Office was in a state of disarray. Trash cans flooded over; dirt was clouding off the wheels of the nutty trucks as the carriers rolled their parcels to the motor pool to prepare for mail delivery. On June 5, the DPS trays got mixed up and carriers were heading out to routes with incorrect DPS letters. Within the next fourteen days, the Union representative was called in regarding a cross-crafting dispute. Three days later, the alarm was triggered at 4:05 a.m. The following Saturday, Louise began her position as the lead sales and service associate. The morning of June 26, the tension between the clerks and myself climaxed as a verbal assault transpired. I waited in the break room for the morning supervisor to arrive via his instructions. Alaina was in window training. July 1, Alaina had returned to work with the unfortunate news she had failed window training and she would not be making regular. I was then informed due to the failure I would be next to go.

July 16, I successfully passed window training. On July 17, I came into work at 4:00 a.m. to throw parcels. After the initial completion of the morning parcels, a shift of aggression went toward Alaina. As we spread DPS on the rural route side, two clerks pushed an A cart of DPS toward her then walked away, leaving her with the entire task of spreading it. The two clerks beckoned me to follow. I declined and assisted in the spreading of DPS. July 25, I requested to see a copy of the customer surveys. August 1, I completed my window training and began my contractual position as the SSDA.

There is a silent epidemic happening in workplaces everywhere. Workplace bullying is wrecking companies and destroying lives. The APWU is a necessary entity in today's postal service to protect hardworking postal workers against injustices. However, it does not discriminate. Bullying tactics are not illegal, and the job security has provided an arena for malevolence.

Upon receiving the news of Alaina's failure at window school was the moment I knew there was something deeper going on in the background. I live my life by a moral compass, and I will not deviate to survive. I will not watch it happen to someone else. These behaviors have names, and as much as the people doing them would like to believe it results from their creativity and wit, they are bully tactics used to carry out individual agendas.

After going through the window training and reading the Sales and Service Associate guide twice cover to cover and taking the test, Alaina is a victim of "misuse of performance appraisal, through plausible deniability." It is the most damaging tactic, and it creates a false self-identity for the victim on the receiving end. The echoed reason for her failing was the "language barrier."

Once I suspected there may be problems that pose as a threat to my career, I felt the wise decision to protect myself was to read manuals. Disorder and chaos can be restored with work ethic and persistence; abuse can be stopped with a courageous by stander. Only literature and documentation can save a soul in the midst of malevolence in the hands of the wicked. These are simply facts and are non-accusatory. When corruption finds its way into positions of power and agendas shift from a universal one (the Postal Mission) to a personal one is when a universal path to success becomes bombarded with wolves.

From August 1 until now, there have been three clerks starting their employment at Newark. I have watched carefully to ensure they are safe from any target placed upon their backs. A bully measures their worth by the body count of the victims with the misfortune of starting their careers in their view finder. I do not even have to research to know with certainty there has been a swinging door of individuals come and go throughout the years. Bullying in the work-place seeks to exploit, blackmail, and control the environment around them. Their use of tactics is inventive and destructive. They harbor on the insecurities of others; they play on the incompetence of management by giving them false and skewed information to disrupt due diligence. They are intelligent and dangerous to all who pose a risk to his/her way of life. They do not care about the success of the post office nor the people around them, only the continued freedom to control and manipulate through abusive tactics.

I decided to message the Area 2 POOM when I felt the Newark postmaster had lost control of his environment. There have been no attempts at mediation for reasons that are a mystery. I wrote an observation report in which I e-mailed the Area 2 POOM a couple of weeks ago. The only individual with any insight on this is TED. I knew my mental status was the only possible attack that could be attempted by any-one in which I am prepared.

In the three-ring binder, I have printed out all text messages between myself and management staff. Additional evidence to support my character is four essays I have written in the name of improving our organization. I made an inspirational video promoting the Post office. Additionally, I have completed nearly forty classes on the Hero website to help me become a more knowledgeable individual in postal affairs.

In summary, I will share my honest belief to what has transpired, I have exhausted all other possibilities, and I cannot see any other puzzle pieces that fit so perfectly. I have no vendetta against anyone. My mind is stimulated by numbers and problem-solving. I will share the current state of the Newark Post Office and its supervisors. Last, I will suggest a solution. Do I have your permission to read the following?

These remarks are not proven. They are opinions and reasonable explanations behind factual events that have transpired. The following information is for possibilities and should not be taken literally. Do I have your permission to read the following?

I believe upon arriving at the Newark Post Office, there was a collaborated effort into seeing Postmaster Jay fail for reasons of control of their environment. After gaining confidence that a postmaster's position was an option was the moment Postmaster Jay brought in Louise as the LSSA. As documented in my observation report, I feel the decision or matters pertaining to the decision soured the employee Thelma.

The next step was to eliminate anything that might pose a potential risk to dishonest actions and that was putting Alaina back in the back of the line to become a contractual employee. Robin, a PSE who has known Jay prior, came and worked at the Newark Post Office. I was next in line to go to window training. Having caught wind of the perceived injustice to Alaina, I arrived at window training to make a failing outcome a literal impossibility.

The current state of the Newark Post Office is functional and in a state of stable operation. I continue to take the full force of the abuse keeping the individuals here who see it as a demented game of control busy to safeguarding the hearts and minds of the incoming personal that our organization so desperately needs.

The supervisors are paralyzed and lack the fortitude to act through no fault of their own. The social consequences are devastating. Two out of the four have fallen into the trap of temptation with the false sense of safety provided by their mentor.

Ted possesses the knowledge and can run this post office as of currently. He is a man of integrity.

I recommend removing Jay, transferring Thelma.

I relinquish the burden of possessing this information into your hands. I lack the will and desire to invest any further intervention. My actions are based solely on the good of our postal system and the protection of all individuals who work in this facility. All attacks on myself will continue to be documented and recorded. I will act as I always do by the book and without bias. I am happy to answer any questions.

Bradley Grubb exhaled. "Okay, Joel, at ease…"

CHAPTER 12

Universal Path to Success; Bombarded with Wolves

In hindsight, Grubbs's wisdom to do nothing was the correct choice. Or at least nothing that I could see in my position. It could have been the case he did a lot more for me then I realized. The truth of the matter was my Letter of Address to the Area 2 POOM was incomplete. When I wrote, "I am unable to see any other puzzle pieces that fit so perfectly," there was more to the puzzle.

Driving back to the Newark Post Office, I felt a sense of relief. My hands are free, and I can just relax, do my job and go home. When I started working for the USPS, I was closing the chapter on a competitive bodybuilding. That was my pastime and hobby. Now that I had completed the learning curve of my duties, I needed something to do in my free time, so I picked up carpentry. It is a useful skill to know, plenty of creative opportunities. Like bodybuilding, it is something that reflected well on my character and could get lost in. It is also something I could chat about socially with some of the guys at work, although only a few had any experience in carpentry.

My friend Mike the custodian was a fellow wood worker, and so was our Postal 1, Sid. I remember drawing out plans for shelfs in my shop and showing them to Mike. He looked at them and said, "Can't you do something simple?" I laughed because he was right.

My plans did not work. Mike was a Vietnam veteran and a collector of silver and gold.

Sid was a God-fearing man who had thirty years in the post office. He would always say, "You're either going up or you're going down." We butted heads a lot but quick to make up. Sid is probably the smartest guy in our entire post office when it comes to crystalized IQ. (Facts and knowledge acquired throughout time.) He is a postal encyclopedia. The best dad in the world, he loved his kids that's for sure.

I pulled back in the Newark Post Office, and things were quiet the rest of the day and the next. I knew what was coming, The wrath of vengeance. I did not have any fear anymore because I brought it to the next level up. I resolved an issue without the Union.

I genuinely felt sadness in my heart. Writing this now, I feel dejected. I could not foresee events that followed, but the response was easy, and I knew the destination of the supervisors. It was a path to nowhere. A post office does the same thing every day. We were increasingly getting better, and the incline would continue to improve. That, however, has a stopping point because without leadership roles to give the employees work-related goals to aspire to and performance measures, they are just sitting there in silence counting the seconds; that is no way to live. When I talked to the POOM, that could have been an opportunity to go straight. That is not what happened.

> Do not rejoice when your enemy falls, and let not
> be glad when he stumbles, lest the lord see it and
> be displeased, and turn away his anger from him.
> (Proverbs 24:14–20)

Accountability Cart S.O.P.
Events Log 10/23/2019.

In order to continuing the Postal Services commitment to fostering and achieving a work and learning environment that respects and values a diverse workforce I feel this will help our ongoing effort to promote innovation, creativity, productivity and growth that enables a broadening of existing concepts.

October 23, 2019, I entered the post office at my usual start time, 10:00 a.m. I removed empty bulk mailing equipment and began transferring them to the truck. Things were quiet, and I waited in anticipation. I could only imagine what was going to happen next, although I was hoping for peace. I hoped we could put our differences aside and come together as a team.

Newark would be the best post office in the country. At 3:00 p.m., Louise was called back to the postmaster quarters for a meeting. Bernie and I were at the window taking care of customers. I still repeatedly asked to see the customer surveys, but the response was there weren't any. Customers would often ask if I had seen the survey they had left, and I had to tell them, "I have not." Louise would be infuriated by this. I had not smelled alcohol on Louise since the observation report, but her eyes were glassy. Her moods would fluctuate. From irritable to manically happy broadcasting and shouting.

Theft prevention and detection expert David Harris speaks about common behaviors within people who commit acts of embezzlement often do so to support a substance abuse habit. They have a feeling of entitlement and view the relationship between the boss and themselves as a partnership or 50/50 ownership (*The Hard Reality of Dental Embezzlement with David Harris,* https://youtu.be/Ve-QoVqHua0).

The meeting ended at 3:25 p.m., and I noticed something was wrong with Louise. It was like the she had been unchained. I was called in the office.

Jay said, "You are to sign for the arrow keys from the carriers as they enter the building."

"Yes, sir, carriers start coming back from 3:00 p.m. to 6:00 p.m. Do you want me to stay by the cart and wait for each one?" I asked.

"No. You are to continue to do your duties and sign for the arrow keys as they come back."

"What if I'm at the window, sir?"

"You are to sign for the keys."

"Would it be okay if I went through the accountable cart and signed the keys off at the end of the night?'

Ted nodded.

"No!" said Jay as the carriers came back.

"Can management provide an SOP so I can better understand how I can perform the requested task?" I asked.

"Yes, we will get you an SOP."

Everything was an attempt to gain checks and balances. It made me extremely conscious of my actions. I wrote everything down that I did. One of the things I enjoy about my job is that there is no downtime. I am busy from the moment I arrive to the moment I return. Having read proper operations of the accountable cart in *Handbook M-41* pp. 33–35 and the Postal Operations Manual, I knew the accountability cart and procedures and the fashion in which it was handled at Newark was completely wrong. Additionally, I had a paper that Luke signed off the moment AJ had put the arrow keys in the pencil pouches.

After the carriers had come back and departed for the night, I began going through and conducting a thorough check of accountable items to bring to the attention of the postmaster.

Figure 1. Missing arrow keys.

Figure 2. Unsecured revenue.

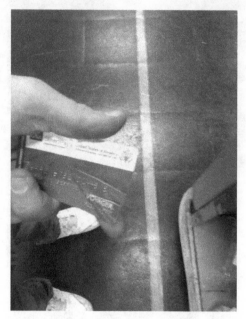

Figure 3. Damaged gas card.

As I conducted checks, Luke started texting on his phone.
Luke said, "Uh. Joel? What ya doing?"

"I'm accounting for the items on the accountable cart, Luke."

He really was not sure what to do or say. In the postal service, everything we do has a Standard of Procedure. One thing the Union does is ensure management abides by those SOP. I am neither an advocate or an obiter of the Union. I am grateful for them, but when people are placed in a certain environment with clearly defined text how to perform job duties, you have to assume one of two things:

Management knows the job duties.

Employees will do them.

The expertise of the individual becomes transparent through their actions. I have no idea how to manipulate the environment to aid in successful continual theft. Throughout the months, it became very transparent that everything that happened was likely for that reason. These behaviors came at a cost to the postal service—the honest people who were not involved (such as Alaina) whose careers were sideswiped.

After a complete check, I made my way to the computer. I had written down multiple accountable items that were missing or damaged. I was given instructions that I was responsible for those items and felt it was wise to e-mail the POOM.

Luke approached. "Joel, it's time to go home now."

"Okay, Luke. Let me send this, and I'll head on out." Luke left. I began typing the discrepancies.

> 4 missing arrow keys.
> C-10 gas card was inoperative.
> C-6 gas card was taped to accountable cart.
> C-26 has no gas card.
> C-34 key slot was empty.
> C-45 gas card was broken.
> C-54 had no gas card.
> R-1 gas card was taped to shelf...

The list went on. Five minutes after Luke departed, I heard the door open and he returned. "Postmaster Jay said I had to leave when you leave." I finished up the e-mail and went to Send. At that very moment, the door opened just seconds before I hit the Send button. Jay came storming in, slightly out of breath. I froze.

Jay asked, "Are you off the clock?"

"Yes, sir."

"Leave the building! Why are you in my building?"

Jay was enraged, I was prepared for anything. At that moment, I smelled the alcohol. He could tell I had, and his demeanor went from offense to defense. I became observant and submissive.

"I was writing a letter to the POOM, sir."

"No! Shut it down! Go home." He looked at Luke. "You stay."

I did exactly what he said. On my way out, Jay shouted, "It is a violation of the security of the building!"

I have been humbled in my life. Talents, intelligence—all the gifts we receive in this world do not excuse us from immoral personal decisions. If anything, the responsibility to walk righteously is elevated. I learned in my twenties that it did not matter how much good

I did in my life; if I adopted anything that was unbecoming, it was all for nothing. It only takes one drop of poison to ruin a batch of apple cider. I cheated on my wife. It did not matter what the circumstances were. I was married; I cheated.

October 24, 2019, I entered work and saw Sid, our Postal 1. Sid is the nicest guy, and I felt comfortable talking to him freely about things. He was sixty years old and had seen many things in the postal service. I handed Sid a copy of the accountability cart observation report and wanted to know what his thoughts were on the "suggested solution page." I rarely ever documented something without suggesting a solution to fix it. My goal was to improve, not persecute. I told Sid in a casual way of the events that transpired. Sid had been informed to relay the information to Jay, and that is what he did.

Jay called me in the office. "What is this I hear of you telling people I was drunk last night?"

"I told Sid…"

"That's defamation of my name!"

"Were you?"

"I had one glass of wine!"

That was an uncomfortable time for me because I wanted so bad for Jay to succeed. I was put in this strange place of protecting myself while wishing the ones who were on the offense. Well. It was never about win or lose, or me versus them. There was no competition. It was career suicide for them and a lot of unwanted documenting for me. The last thing I wanted to do after a ten-hour day was go home and write it down. Again, the postal service was the same thing over and over.

"I would not have said that, Jay…" I paused. "I want you to succeed! I am in your corner 100 percent. I always have been."

EVENTS LOG/OBSERVATION REPORT 10/24/2019

10:00 A.M.- Clocked in

10:20 A.M.- Summoned by Postmaster to conduct meeting pertaining 10/23/2019 events.

11:00 A.M.- Continued to take empty equipment to trailer.

11:30 A.M. Assisted in offloading of UPS truck.

12:00 - Placed Placards on equipment in preparation of dispatching out going Parcels.

12:15 - Prepared out going parcels for 12:30 early dispatch.

12:47 - Clocked out for 1-hour mandatory lunch.

13:30- Sean instructed me to throw UPS Parcels in between dispatch duties. (See attached)

13:47- Returned from lunch.

13:47- Performed early 569 scans.

14:30 - Conducted mid-day parcel assortment in preparation for dispatch.

15:30 Completed loading of 1st truck

15:45- 1st Truck departed for Columbus.

16:30 - 2nd truck departed for Columbus.

17:00 - Performed end of day scans.

17:15 - Performed Parcel sorting in preparation for final dispatch.

18:30- Final truck departed to Columbus facilities.

18:31- Put accountable cart away in Postal safe room.

18:35- Performed final 569 parcel select scans.

19:00 – Clock out.

The remainder of the meeting went well; we discussed some possible changes to the dispatch desk area that would improve our accountability. Jay told me to go out and get everything set up and to come and get him. He did not read my notes, though, so I gave a copy to our maintenance man because it pertained to his area of expertise. I proceeded with my daily task.

After helping UPS unload the parcels into the containers, I staged them as I usually do, finished the placards for dispatch, and clocked out for lunch. While on lunch, I was reading the Employee Labor Manual. That's when I witnessed Louise begin to sort through junk mail. (We call this Undeliverable Bulk Business Mailings, like advertisements. Occasionally a first-class letter would be found.) This broke the pattern of normalcy, and I began to pay attention to what was going on. Parcels scans always take priority over UBBM. She had gone back to the window, and then Robin came out and sorted UBBM. Then so did our newest employee, John. I heard Luke's shoes clicking; I knew what he was going to say or was told to say.

"Hey Joel," said Luke, "in between dispatch duties, how about we get those parcels thrown?"

I was red. Not because he gave me a lawful order—it was 100 percent lawful—but because I had to spend another night at my computer typing.

"Delay of mail through misdelegation of duties! US Code 1703," I said.

Luke did not reply. A few minutes later, the clerks who were sorting through the UBBM scanned the parcels that were staged.

The following day was Friday, October 25, and something strange happened that day. There was no tension. The only thing that was unusual was that Thelma went and worked on the window for forty-five minutes and went home. She waited until the other clerks left, though. It was an uneventful day. I asked Ted about other post offices and if they were similar to this one. Despite all the recent activity, Jay still wanted me there. I always figured he appreciated my work ethic and knew I never would sabotage postal operations. The only thing I could connect to the easy day to was Louise having the day off.

OCTOBER 28th, 2019 EVENTS/OBSERVATION REPORT.

10:00 – Clock in, began moving FSS carts/empty equipment to the truck.

11:30 – Assisted in the unloading of UPS Parcels.

11:40 – Clerk Lance Notifies me of a scheduled passport arrival. (See attached)

11:45- Postmaster gives instructions to depart home to pick up my Acceptance agent number.

11:50-I log into RSS.

12:00 – RSS Opens drawer.

12:05 – I perform passport services.

12:25- I gather first set of parcels for early dispatch.

12:35- I-wheel early dispatch Parcels out to dock area. (See attached.)

13:00 – I began spreading Marketing mail to assigned routes. (3/8 skids)

14:30- I inquire when a good time to take lunch would be. No clear answer was given.

14:45 – I conduct Midday Parcel assortment from Heath office with parcels from front.

15:50 – First truck departs to Processing Plant.

1645 – Second truck departs to processing plant.

17:05 – Perform end of day box scans/assort end of day parcels.

1830 - Final truck departs to Columbus.

19:00 – Place accountable cart in Postal Safe.

19:05 – Perform 569 Scans (123 scans)

19:45- Spread Marketing mail

19:50 – Supervisor Sean asks inquires about the status of the Marketing mail. (See attached)

20:00 – Clean dispatch desk, clock out, depart.

On Monday, October 28, I walked into a destroyed dispatch area. Absolutely wrecked. The initial cleanup of dispatch takes me forty-five minutes. Whenever the morning clerks wrecked it, it would take me ninety minutes. On occasion, it was so bad it would take me until noon. UPS parcel bags, USPS parcel bags, empty boxes…sometimes they would unwrap plastic tubs that had been prepared to go to the processing plant. It got creative. It crossed the line of reasonable doubt. I cannot say with 100 percent certainty, but I would suspect they were bringing in empty equipment from the dock and placing it in the dispatch area. That is crazy from a multitude of perspectives because I would just wheel it back where it went on the dock. The question that would haunt me for the months to come was "Why?" Not in the regard that I wanted to be liked, but where was this resentment coming from? There was no social contact. We were only around each other for maybe an hour. I would work as hard as I could from the moment I arrived until the moment I left. So why?

At 11:30 a.m., the UPS driver arrived. His name was Matt. I unloaded the bags, and I began to dump them. Bernie came out and got my attention. "We have a passport appointment here." I told Matt to just leave them on the dock and I would take care of it when I got a minute. Louise was on vacation that week Robin had been sent to Heath. Thelma was throwing parcels. Bernie was certified, but Louise had given him the answers to the passport test. (It's extremely difficult.) I think they were just trying to get the numbers of certified people up.

The time was 11:35 a.m., and the couple had made the appointment for 11:30. Logging into retail system software took several minutes. The couple were standing there, patiently waiting. There was no excuse for their scheduled wait time. After my system came up, I put my cash drawer in. "I am so sorry," I apologized to the couple. Then it hit me. I had left my passport number at home! I apologized again and ran back to the office to see if Jay had my accepting agent's number. He did not.

"Well, the couple is out there!" I said. "Do you want me to go home and grab my accepting agent's number?"

"Yes, go get it!"

I literally ran out to my Jeep renegade and floored it a mile down the road to my house.

With my book in hand, I ran back to the window. At that point, the couple had been waiting for thirty minutes regardless of the four qualified passport clerks we had present. I knew what they were doing, but that was no excuse. A customer had made an appointment and was waiting. I began passport services with my tail in between my legs. I took care of four passports that day. After turning a customer away once (I had to transport overloading parcels and prepare them for a truck due in ten minutes), I ran back to collect the UPS that had been left on the dock. What I saw was horrific. The morning clerks had obliterated the loading dock. I could not even see the concrete. It was a mixture of parcel carts, cages, and UPS bags.

I said out loud, "*I must be in the fu**ing Twilight Zone!*" I hardly curse. I could…not…believe it.

I entered back inside and requested Ted and Luke come look at the loading dock. Ted was a mild-mannered person. Luke was a good supervisor. I would say one thing he lacks, if I'm allowed to be hypercritical, because there are many things I lack, but if I had to pick one thing, that would be he often doesn't have the greatest tact when approaching situations.

The three of us walked out on the loading dock, and I asked, "Does this look normal to you?"

It was interesting looking at Luke's face. I was looking at his face while writing this, and it was a type of look that was seeing something for the first time that was unsettling. I saw his brain was processing new information and formulated thoughts of shock and searching for what to do. Ted was wearing a green polo. He had one arm across his chest and the other resting on top of it, extending up to his face, while he worked things out in his mind. Ted was a deep thinker; he always had a hand-face fixation when he was at a loss or perturbed. That is something I never saw out of Jay. The eyes tell a story. When someone is deep in thought or searching for solutions, they disappear in their minds. You see it in the eyes. I ask questions all the time, and I look in the eyes of the person I am asking. I listen to their voice; when you are around people every day you know their body language. It is unique for every person. Occasionally, I could formulate some type of compelling argument for Louise that would cause some type of reconsideration or a new perspective on things that would cause her to disappear in cognition, but her beliefs or her reasoning for doing certain things were so concreted. I saw her snap out of it and say, "I choose happiness" Happiness is not merely a choice. It is a combination of choices that brings about well-being. "I choose happiness." I thought to myself, *At what cost? More importantly, the cost of who or what?*

Ted broke out of his trance. "Yep, it must be the new guy. Don't worry, I'm going to talk to him." We had a new PSE start employment. His name was Tyler. Mild-mannered kid. Nineteen years old, liked to hunt.

Luke said, "That's a fire hazard!" I regained order on the loading dock and continued.

We had incorporated an early dispatch of parcels at that time. A driver from Columbus would come around 1:00 p.m. to collect first-class and priority parcels. I wheeled the BMUs to the dock and saw it: eight skids of Every Door Direct Mail, the advertisement mail the public typically dislikes flooding their mailbox.

Panic and frustration began to set in. These things must go out by Tuesday. If I could not get them spread to the routes, then the risk of failing the deadline became a real possibility. My heart rate began to elevate. I saw the pallet jack and took the first one it. Each skid weighed an average of 1,500 pounds. I looked at the top layer of bundles.

"C-34." Like football drills, I began chopping my feet to put these massive things into motion. Through the swinging doors I went, over to C-34's case. From my back pocket, I removed a box cutter and slit the plastic wrap that was holding the bundles together. I grabbed the first two bundles within the unit and put them at the C-34. It was a workout.

Once getting through the first skid of EDDMs, my blue USPS polo started showing signs of wetness from sweat. I peeled my top and got the second skid. At 2:30 p.m., I had to stop. I managed to complete three skids. I approached Luke and asked when he would like me to take my lunch. I could not get an answer out of him.

Something I was overly critical on was choosing my words carefully. I often refer to the Bible in this book, reason being whether someone is a believer or not, there hasn't been a book I've read that's given me more wisdom surrounding how I should act in the midst of a malevolent environment.

Do not give what is holy to the dogs, and do not throw your pearls before swine, or they will trample them under their feet and turn and tear you to pieces. (Matthew 7:6)

I could not talk to anyone, not even Sid. If I said, "Today it is busy," that would translate to "Joel thinks everyone is lazy." It was a continuous search for ammunition and dogmatism. They saw it as a battle, and I did not want to fight. The only casualty would be the efficiency of unit operations and, ultimately, postal revenue. The ability for the USPS to make money is what feeds the families of the

USPS employees. To engage in that behavior would mean I willfully contributed to actions that jeopardized the future of 630,000 people. That is the big picture. The magnitude of that undeniable fact resonated with me, and the responsibility to do my job drove my behavior. I had to fight. Not only for my own life and reputation but for an immeasurable number of people. To look at it in any other way was damning.

I worked ten straight hours. After I clocked out, I made my way home and sat at my computer to write down an awful day.

OCTOBER 31st, 2019 EVENTS/OBSERVATION REPORT.

10:00 – Clock in, began moving FSS carts/empty equipment to the truck.

11:30 – Assisted in the unloading of UPS Parcels.

11:40 – Prepare Placards for Dispatch Mail.

11:45- Noticed written message left by Supervisor Mary Grace. (See attached)

12:00- I request Paycheck from Supervisor Lance.

12:05 - Supervisor Lance informs me of the new Surveys. (See attached)

12:15 – Supervisor Mary Grace Informs me of a U.B.B.M. Deficiency (See attached)

12:25- I gather first set of Parcels for early dispatch.

12:35- I conduct sorting of Parcels from U.P.S.

12:47- I clock out for lunch.

13:47- I return from lunch.

14:45 – I conduct Midday Parcel assortment from Heath office with parcels from front.

15:40 – I discuss earlier events with Supervisor Lance. (See attached)

15:50 – First truck departs to Processing Plant.

1645 – Second truck departs to processing plant.

17:05 – Perform end of day box scans/assort end of day parcels.

17:45 – Conduct 569 Scans.

19:00 – clock out/Perform final duties.

19:10 – Final Truck arrives. Late arrival was due to traffic.

One of the biggest things I wanted was something to validate my performance. I wanted it for motivation and my own self-esteem. How someone views themselves in their heads is rarely reflective of reality. An individual who has narcissistic personality disorder views themselves as God's gift to the earth but lives a life of poor decision-making and malice, unable to connect the two having anything to do with their current position in life. They are resentful and entitled.

I have gone to the deepest depths to try to understand myself. Where do I fit in the world? How can I contribute? I question my own place. My own feelings for feeling a certain way. I ask, "Does this bother me because I feel entitled to receive it? Or because I should receive it?" The failing of my business was a result of me engaging sexually with girls that came to my gym. Nothing else mattered. The consequences of what happened as a result changed my psychology. The point at which it happened was right at the point where my life was not completely ruined. If it would have happened in my forties, there would not be any coming back. That would be my legacy. It's relevant because in order to inspire change or be influential, you must have some type of credentials; otherwise, I appear to be crazy.

I didn't have a choice when it came to my actions within the Newark Post Office. It's as if God placed me in the most hostile and corrupt environment and said, "If you want validity behind your words, then fix this or continue living with what you had bestowed upon yourself years before." If the USPS were flawless, it would have been simple to climb the ladder by performance and creativity. It just wasn't, and I passed up the opportunity to change careers—selfish? Maybe. The morally right thing to do? Without a doubt.

MEMORANDUM OF UNDERSTANDING

In my Letter of Address to the Postal Operations Area Manager, I stated, "I will address all issues by the book and without bias." It darkens my world to put forth in motion actions that have the potential to derail someone's career path. However, I demand three things: You act with virtue. You act with integrity. And you act with improving this organization. If I were in a position of influence, I would expect my subordinates to ask that of me. I, along with many others, want to come to work with a peace of mind. That demands a level of insight and continuous self-development on your part to be able to adapt and overcome all problems that the postal service faces. You have my unwavering support and commitment for all decisions made in the name of progress and unit cohesion. I do not want to fast-track my career; I have no ulterior motive. I, however, have a son to think about, and I am employed by an organization that is in a state of financial emergency. This is the final written document I will provide to the Newark management staff. I will not discuss among peers, and I recommend this letter stay in the privacy of the leadership team. You have my 100 percent support in the name of improving this organization.

I did not send anything.

CHAPTER 13

Desperation and Doubt

The management team were all relatively new to the Newark Post Office; they had one thing in common. Many of them were coming from the same office—Westerville. I began to ask myself if in fact there was a simple way to steal money with a likelihood of continuing. Would it in fact be an occurrence that would manifest itself everywhere? A more direct question would be, is this possibly a Newark problem? Or a postal problem? The ultimate question: "Has this contributed to the demise of the USPS? Lastly, why hasn't it been resolved?

On April 30, 2019, a full committee hearing took place over the financial condition of the USPS. Over the course of several months, I have listened to it several times, initially once a day. Pauses in words, sarcasm in questions, body language in the congress members, Body language in Postmaster Brennan when presented with certain questions (https://youtu.be/-1oX8Cfi0AQ).

One thing I asked myself, if they know a lot of it is related to theft, why doesn't she say it? Patrick Donahue was the outgoing postmaster general before Brennan. When he tried to switch the USPS to five-day delivery, there was a slew of protest by postal workers. "Yo-ho, Donahue's got to go!" the postal workers chanted and shouted. That was the end of Donahue's legacy, being run out by the men and woman he worked for. They were protecting their shark food. The congressional meeting was based off findings a task force team had discovered (the divers) in the internal controls regarding the USPS financial system. Congress men lynch gave me the next clue at: 1:16:40.

"The postal service now and forever has worked their system off of stamps."

Ted stepped down as the stamp stock custodian, and AJ took over. After listening to Mr. Lynch's comments, I looked for anything that would give me insight to see if that was how they were doing it. Multiple stock transfers a day occurred from the unit reserve to the retail floor stock. Upon logging into retail system software, a notification would occur, saying, "Pending stock transfer." The amount that was being transferred was more than what we were doing in sales.

I did not investigate it past that point. My mind became tired. Christmas was nearing, and I shifted my focus from studying to the Christmas season approaching.

Stacey had recently returned from 204b school, and I always thought Stacey was a good person. I think people are products of their environment. I remember one morning, as we scanned parcels, I was talking about group behaviors and conforming to a belief system shared by a group of people. It's called *group think*.

Thelma asked, "Why didn't you conform?"

"Well…" I replied, "because I'm self-actualized."

"What does that mean?"

"It's the point in time where an individual realizes the potential within themselves that's present in everyone."

Once you find that, it's hard to lose because it usually happens when you reach a level of success past the norm. Your beliefs drive your actions.

A reason it is so important to solve the problem of accountability and internal controls is because any office that may be corrupted will only yield more corruption. This problem works like a virus and spreads. Stacey came back from 204 B School unscathed. It's a look of innocence and freedom one possesses when they do not have to constantly be covering their tracks.

I remember when they turned her but the decision to maintain integrity bares consequences. People begin life in the postal service genuine. It is a transformation that occurs. I would analogize it to using a drug for the first time. Handing someone a fist full of cash with the guarantee of discretion and continuance is an ordeal that a normal person cannot hide. It changes someone's physiology, and behaviors become centered more for checks and balances and control. The Christmas season was close enough to us that parcel volume began to increase.

NOVEMBER 11, 2019. EVENTS LOG.

10:00 – Clocked in began moving empty equipment to the trailer.

10:30- Inquired with ▓▓▓▓▓ for direction pertaining to Holiday tasks that needed completed. **See attached.**

11:00 – Spread outgoing phonebooks to appropriate routes.

11:30 – Assisted UPS Driver in offloading parcels.

12:00 – Continued spreading phone books.

12:15- Assisted in throwing UPS Parcels. (117 units)

12:47 – Clocked out for lunch.

13:47- Returned from lunch.

13:47 – Performed mid-day dispatch.

14:00 – Gathered Parcels from SSK cage area.

14:30- scanned whiskey river prepaid accepted (160 scans)

14:45 – I suggest ▓▓▓▓▓ make a list of additional task she wanted completed.

15:05- First truck arrived. See attached.

15:30- Perform end of day scans.

15:45- Conduct final dispatch/truck departs.

16:00- I perform 569 parcel scans.

16:20 -Carrier returns with additional Parcels.

16:25- I set up a second dispatch area.

17:00- Final truck departs to processing plant.

17:10 – Spread phone books.

17:50 ▓▓▓▓▓ informs me she wishes to leave See attached.

I volunteered to work on Veterans Day; Stacy was the holiday supervisor. Aware of the recent changes, I suspected she would try to gain a checks and balances stronghold. I had to be incredibly mindful of my actions because I would be the only one in the building with her at some point during the night. I entered inside the post office and made my way to the dispatch desk. Stacey was wearing a red Ohio State sweatshirt; Alaina and Robin were scanning parcels. I placed my personal belongings at the dispatch desk and walked over to see if Stacey had any instructions regarding to what she wanted me to do for the holiday tasks. She left abruptly.

"Robin, do you know what was going on?" I asked.

"I'm not sure," she said. "I've been here since 5:00 a.m. I'm leaving here in an hour."

Robin was a hard worker, in her forties and a good person; I liked Robin. I carried on until Stacey gave me directions. I began with the FSS carts. Shortly after, I spotted Stacey and approached to greet her. "Hi, Stacey, is there anything going on today pertaining to the holiday schedule?"

"What do you mean?"

"Well, what needs to be done? What do you want me to do?"

"Just do dispatch…"

A few moments later, she approached. "I want you to spread all these phonebooks to the cases."

There were many phonebooks. Each case had one phonebook for each address on their routes. There are around sixty-three thousand people in Newark. Matt arrived with UPS and by that time we knew each other well and became friends. I walked out to the loading dock.

Matt said, "What's up, man?"

"Oh, not too much. They have you working on Veterans Day, huh?"

Matt laughed. "Oh yeah, you know it."

I staged the UPS parcels next to the ones that had arrived from our processing plant earlier that morning.

Humans being have the innate ability to sense danger in the environment. A large contributor pertaining to my memory over the events that transpired at Newark is largely due to the sympathetic nervous system being activated. It's what creates flashbulb memories. A challenge for me was to not return the aggression with aggression. Only the postal service suffers. I continued to spread phone books for another five minutes. Stacey stopped me, instructing me to throw the UPS parcels. After 118 scans, I went to lunch and prepared for a long day.

The biggest factor in any hierarchical construct is competence. If an individual possess authority over a group, a universally recognized goal must be present. The only appropriate goal is the Postal Mission and contributing to the growth of the USPS. Performance measures and praise reinforces the pursuit of the goal. The most detrimental phenomenon in any organization occurs when local leadership develops personal agendas that do not align with their employers. As a result, subordinates suffer. It's inevitable.

What I suspected would happen with Stacey is at that particular time, she would desire to be influential. Given her authority over me, she would direct me to do whatever deficiencies she saw in the current environment on that particular day. I would have a day filled with "Do this" commands, but that's not leadership. Its maddening for the subordinate because there must be some sense of direction and independency pertaining to tasks. The value of results is often replaced with the value of being obeyed by the individual in the authoritative position. Authority demands insight and integrity in order to be effective.

I returned from lunch and performed my midday tasks. Stacey instructed me to scan parcels that had come in from one of our customers who shipped through eBay. After conducting several tasks that Stacey instructed me to do, I suggested she make a list for me instead of following me around.

This angered Stacey. Upon arrival of the first truck, she began giving me further instructions. "Isn't there a blue box outside of post offices that gets scanned?"

"What are you talking about?"

I could not understand what she was saying because I was responsible for doing end-of-day scans in our blue box, but there was another truck coming.

"You know, the blue box that gets scanned every day," she said.

I had no desire to banter with her. I performed end-of-day duties and dispatched the mail.

The mail had been dispatched, and end-of-day scans were completed; however, there was a carrier still out that soon would bring back parcels. I had to set up a second dispatch and redo the placards. At 5:50 p.m., Stacey wanted to leave early, and we left for the evening. The following morning, I approached Stacey and handed her the document of events that had taken place the day prior.

It fascinated me, the reaction of the supervisors when I gave them these papers. I think seeing things in print had some type of profound effect on them. Someone who is committing crimes may do so justifying it to protect their sense of self with ego defense mechanisms:

- I work too hard.
- It was done to me.
- I deserve this.

The papers themselves induced so much emotional anger. It was as if they were victims and life was out to get them.

A few moments later, Stacey walked back to me, furious. "Now you're putting words into my mouth?"

Tim was there with her.

"No…" I said.

Stacey's eyes began to water, and I thought to myself. *Oh, Lord…* I looked at Tim and his reactions went from observer/recorder to a more empathetic position, as if he were listening to his teenage daughter talk about a fight she had had with a boy at school. I walked away. I did not know how to react to it.

Later that month, I received word that my good friend from high school passed away. He passed away on November 14, 2019. I inquired with management to have the day off. Jay was awarded the postmaster's position at the Newark Post Office. His celebration party was at the same restaurant, on the same day, November 24, 2019, that the gathering of my childhood friends and I chose to go before we departed for our passed brother's calling hours.

December 1, 2019, the post office was nearing immaculate condition. Anyone I had made friends with was targeted or turned. Thelma and Louise had worked their magic. Any carrier that showed any amount of friendship to me would receive increased workloads and pivots (additional mail to be carried on top of their routes). Christmas was approaching, and the dawn of a new challenge was among us. I had not experienced a busy season at a level 21 office. I told Jay, "You have my unwavering support." I would never jeopardize the postal mission. If a postmaster's goals coincide with that, they have my support. Personal feelings play no factor. I work for the USPS and no one else. I had heard horror stories of the incredible volume that Christmas brought in, and I was excited to test my capabilities.

Our Christmas stamps arrived, and I had received another involuntary glimpse of insight. It seemed as if every time I stopped looking for some type of answer that explained the instability of the environment, something would manifest itself that forced me to continue my path to competence. I never would have noticed if Louise had not written in big giant letters on the box "MERRY X-MAS" with a large smiley face. It was so arrogant and egregious. I felt my blood begin to boil. The supervisors worshipped her. They obeyed her without question or evaluation. She was a contractual employee who fell under the union protection. The submissiveness warranted concern. When looking for evidence to a crime, there must be factual events that support an allegation.

Rule 401. Test for Relevant Evidence

Evidence is relevant if

a) it has any tendency to make a fact more or less probable than it would be without the evidence; and

b) the fact is of consequence of determining the action.[1]

The lines began to connect. Louise had a philatelic bag with a George Washington stamp on it. Three to six clerks were rotated throughout the day on the windows. The majority of evenings between 4:00 p.m. and 4:45 p.m., a supervisor would be called up to the window or a supervisor would follow Louise in the women's restroom immediately after she exited or somewhere out of plain sight. There had not been one group talk discussing goals and unit cohesion by management to clerks in the last six months, open and public conflict between the prior T-7 and the postmaster without explanation. Every factual event was supportive of an illegal action: theft.

What many employees fail to see is many dubious events that they experience in the past are more than likely a direct consequence of illegal activities; within bargaining employees, behaviors counter-productive to performance standards are not suggestive of stealing. Similar behaviors in managerial positions certainly are.

I printed off *F-101 Field and Accounting Procedures* and *F-1 Accounting and Reporting Policy*. I began the learning curve of a finan-cial system that only a handful of people in the world are subject matter experts on.

Later that week, I approached Jay and asked him where the 3977 duplicate key envelopes[2] were located.

He looked up at me, perturbed. "Oh, you're studying that now?"

"I want to see them."

"Why are you studying that, Joel?"

"Because I want to know."

"No, you don't!"

He took me back to the safe room and showed me one of the envelopes round dated and signed *Mark Jones 2012*. I wanted to ensure if I locked up the metal filing cabinet on my unit, Louise couldn't get in my drawer and remove stamps while I was in the back dispatching mail. If it were the case that multiple people were engaging in illegal activities, then if the issue ever came in question by authorities, my name and reputation would be on the chopping block. I presumed Louise justified it on the grounds that no persecu-tion would come to anyone so she wasn't hurting anyone.

The volume of parcels began to steadily increase, and the morning clerks anticipated the coming of Christmas. They would always say to me "Just wait, you'll see." I was so headstrong in my work ethic I felt like they wanted to see me overwhelmed or break, for lack of better words. At Newark we have three trucks that come throughout the day. They haul semi trailers to and from the processing plant. The max volume would be measured by the length of three- to fifty-five-foot beds.

I began getting fatigued at the end of the night do to the increased volume. The closing supervisor would watch me closely, never with any positive words of encouragement. At this point, Luke's attitude began to turn, and I felt his resentment toward me. I was determined to contribute as much as I could to maintaining 100 percent up keep on Christmas volume and parcels. Physical fitness would be the contributing factor.

The following weekend, I went to Walmart and sunk my focus into meal prep and conditioning. I purchased lean turkey, chicken breast, sweet potatoes, asparagus, oatmeal, egg whites, and fitness supplements. I was in the zone. Saturday I would spend all day Ubering, and Sunday was meal prep, laundry, and cleaning. All my thoughts centered around success through the busy season.

On December 9, my alarm was set for 6:00 a.m.

Beep, beep, beep. The alarm sounded. I woke up, drank some preworkout, and let the caffeine set in. At 6:45 a.m., I was dressed, shaved, and began loading my oversized lunch box with premade meals and supplement drinks. At 8:00 a.m., I headed to the gym, playing my favorite workout music maxing the volume. I was determined. Nothing was going to stop me. Entering the gym, I began to feel my heart rate increase. I saw the bench press and began warming up with the 45-pound bar. I repped it twenty times. My next set was 135 pounds. I did ten reps and racked it. I peeled my sweatshirt, revealing the USPS cut T-shirt that I had put on that morning. I kept thinking in my head, *No post office has ever maintained 100 percent during the holiday season. How awesome would it be if Newark was able to pull it off.* Both the rural carriers and the city carriers began to really hustle. The motivation was contagious. They all had great attitudes and their energy motivated me even more. My final set of bench was 225 pounds for ten reps. When I first became employed by the USPS, I was saying my goodbyes to competitive bodybuilding. Being a government worker and starting a new career, I felt anything that didn't contribute to my new life should be put in my past. Bodybuilding fit in that category. I was 250 pounds with abs. It was an adjustment for me because leaving the fitness world, I had to rediscover a new sense of identity. Many things I did to attain the size and strength wasn't legal. As a government worker, I had to abide by the same rules as everyone else, and that pertained to all aspects of my life. Obeying the law was non-negotiable.

I walked into the Newark Post Office, I approached my desk, and I could feel the hatred. It was quiet. I walked over to the dispatch desk and drank my protein and prepared my postworkout vitamins. After, I walked to the bathroom and changed my clothes. Louise had begun her warpath. The inquiry of the duplicate key envelope had ignited another battle. It was carnage. The dispatch area was obliterated, and I instantly went into a cardio pace once clocking in.

I rolled out the purple FSS carts at a vigorous speed. At 11:30 a.m., I was called to put my drawer in. I stopped the removing of empty BME equipment to the truck and put on my blue USPS polo. As I logged into retail system software, I noticed the line of people streaming out the door. I thought to myself, *How in the world? I just saw Josie sorting through UBBM! (ad mail) Did these people all come in at once?* The line took five minutes to clear, and I ran outside to see the UPS truck driver offloading bags upon bags of parcels. Matt had stopped coming to the Newark location for Christmas because his route had picked up so much in volume. UPS rented out box trucks to carry out the delivery of "first- and last-mile" parcels assigned to Newark. That particular day, it was nearly two hundred parcels and bags. Each UPS bag held about as much as a large contractor trash bag would. The bags were filled with smaller boxes and spurs (clothing or smaller items placed in small plastic wrappings or padded envelopes).

I had eight large USPS boxes (large card board boxes that were used as disposable bulk mailing containers, roughly one hundred cubic feet) set up to dump the bags and place the parcels in. As I began unzipping the UPS bags, the bell rang, notifying me the window clerks needed a fourth window clerk to help with customers. I told the UPS worker to just throw the bags on the loading dock and I would take care of it when I returned.

I ran up to the lobby area to discover there was a long line of people out the lobby doors. I was shocked because I had only been gone for ten minutes. I looked at the other window clerks' facial expressions to see signs of panic, stress, excitement—anything that I could see to help me understand what they were witnessing before I came to assist. They were blank and nonchalant. We cleared the line in twelve minutes. I ran back out to the loading dock. The UPS worker had taken the UPS bags and barricaded herself inside the truck. I began to lose my patience.

The worker was a middle-aged woman who had recently became employed with UPS as a temporary worker and was there for the busy season. She had received one day of training, and it was apparent she didn't want to be there. I found an opening through the mound she had created and asked, "Ma'am, why wouldn't you toss the parcels enough away so you could get out?"

I shouldn't have said anything. I sensed what she was doing was more of a spite-centered ordeal, and she was overwhelmed by the workload. I removed the mound and continued dumping UPS parcels from bags. The front window bell rang again.

There is no way, I thought to myself. My blood pressure began to spike. The supervisors were absent in Jay's office. (An excuse that is often vocalized among the management team was "I wasn't there." Whenever I came to work and saw Jay's truck gone, I would prepare myself.) I ran up front, and sure enough, a line was out the door. The frustration showed in my eyes, and the window clerks were cold and emotionless. After clearing the line, I ran back out and stopped to look behind me. Two out of three window clerks followed me out the clerk station entrance and began doing busy work, the work you would do when the post office is slow and absent of customers, work such as checking e-mails, sorting through UBBM. The only person that stayed at the window was John, our newest window clerk. When

John rang the bell, it was for all three of us and not just me. My face turned red.

Customers were having to wait in line over petty, childish actions. I thought to myself, *Where are the supervisors? Why would anyone let this happen? Over a personal vendetta? This is lunacy!* I was furious. I couldn't figure out why Louise had such control. She saw that I had caught wind of what they were doing, and the other two clerks went back to the window. Her mission every day was to enrage me or at least come up with some creative way of holding up task that I had to do. The dispatch position was the most demanding job in the post office. Parcels had to be ready to go out in time for trucks. If, for some reason, I was held up, then Sid, our Postal 1, would have to pick up the slack.

It took me an additional forty-five minutes to unbag and stage the UPS parcels behind the blue hampers. The morning clerks clocked out at 12:30, and the supervisors did not make them stay to throw the large amount of UPS parcels that needed to be finished. During the holiday, an additional truck would come before our 3:30 p.m. truck arrived. At 1:30 p.m., I cocked out for lunch. I took ten minutes to eat and worked through my lunch until 2:30 p.m., when I was able to clock in.

Once clocking in, I furiously prepared a mountain of parcels scattered between nutty trucks, random hampers, and back near the window area. They had to be ready to be dispatched in one hour. The bell rang five minutes after starting. I looked at Postal 1 Sid, shaking my head in disbelief.

Sid said, "*Jesus!* They got three people up there! Your job is the dispatch! Three window clerks is plenty!"

I mirrored his frustration. "What do you want me to do, Sid?"

Luke looked at me and said, "Louise is the T-7. The customers are waiting!"

I thought in my head, *You little weasel...* After returning, I continued to work on sorting the dispatch parcels. Thirty seconds later, she got on the intercom.

"Joel to the window! Joel to the window right now!" called Louise.

My thoughts continued to race. I had to do my job. I didn't go up when Louise called. Luke ran up to the window after having a moment of conflict. Twenty seconds passed. Luke got on the intercom. *"Joel to the window. We got a line out the door!"*

I looked at Jeff and said, "What a sh——t show..." Sid stopped his Postal 1 duties and began doing dispatch. I ran back up to the window, and Louise was on the phone with the retail system software help desk. People in line were enraged. As soon as I logged in to my unit, Louise hung up the phone and began helping customers. We cleared the line in thirty minutes. I sprinted back to the dispatch desk and finished the loading of the first truck just in the nick of time.

Sid approached Luke and said, "Listen, buster! I got my own things to do. He's got to do his dispatch work before anything else!"

When the 4:30 truck arrived, Louise got on the intercom. "Joel to the window! Joel to the window!"

Luke finally stepped in and said, "Joel, you stay here and do dispatch!" He walked up to the lobby and told Louise.

At 5:00 p.m., I prepared to do end-of-day box scans and conduct my closeout of my cash drawer. I went to log in, and the screen read *Incorrect Password*. I tried it again: *Incorrect Password*. One more time... *Incorrect password*. "Your system has been locked out. Please conduct RSS help desk." The thoughts racing in my head were a less commonly used word for a female dog. I called the RSS help desk and was able to get whatever happened to my computer resolved, but the ordeal took thirty minutes.

The time was 5:40, and I was way behind schedule. Louise clocked out, putting on her sunglasses and dancing cheerfully, with her Philatelic handbag swinging from her side. I looked at Luke and said, "I'm sorry, but is the sun out?" It was pitch black outside. I presumed Luke would not make the connection that is well-documented in the psychology world associating crime with masks or sunglasses.

I finished loading the final truck at 6:45 p.m. After all the dispatch tasks were completed, I ate my final meal and headed toward the PASS machine to start the final sprint of the day's completions. I finished the last of the UPS scans at 8:30 p.m. I clocked out and

Ubered until 10:00 p.m. I walked into my apartment, dropped my lunch box on the floor, and climbed into bed exhausted. I was out the moment my head hit the pillow.

The human memory is often inaccurate. I took very good notes throughout the year, and without them, all this would be rendered as foolery and meritless. I think we act in accordance to our own belief system, and our behavior is a reflection of our experiences. Someone who sabotages what's considered socially acceptable conduct will do so with the reinforcing belief system that it was done to them and the person responsible who did it to them had no repercussions. The person gained as a result of malevolence. Often in life, that's the story of an individual. A inability or unwillingness to return evil with evil, resulting in the peril of the person on the receiving end. The value of leadership is so dynamic when it comes to overseeing and preventing these types of occurrences.

The vantage point of how I perceived these things is from a profit-revenue perspective. The USPS is a business. Status and success appeal to me as an individual. With a higher position comes more financial gain, more influence, and ability to do good. That trickles down to my personal life of appealing to a partner who is smart, attractive, and wants to have a family. Then my children will have a higher chance of success in life and so on. The decisions I make on a daily basis transcend and shape my entire future. If I am looking at things from a long-term approach, then it makes the most sense to behave in that exact way the literature describes. The logical solution to fast-tracking my career in the USPS is to become proficient at understanding revenue efficiency and maximization. That doesn't mean derailing people's careers. People do that to themselves. What it means is finding the problems associated with loss and resolving the issue. That is what I am supposed to do.

Having said that, I would be deceiving myself if I proclaimed that the childish games didn't spark some negative emotion and anger. To be frank, it infuriated me. Why couldn't they see what I see? Why are they indulging in such ridiculous behaviors? The truth of the matter is, people are people. The tolerance of personalities lies within the spectrum of revenue loss or revenue gain. Characteristics of an individual determine if the person contributes to the bottom line or taints the bottom line. Dishonesty, substance abuse, and confrontation are all characteristics that taint what every USPS employee is hired to do. If the USPS dies, we all lose.

I documented the last year accurately. It came from a vantage point of fixing a problem. If I took these things personally, I wouldn't have lasted. The conflicts were very stressful, but it held no relevance to how I view myself or confidence in my actions. I believe, given the nature of how our postal units, are set up the problem at Newark is a problem at every office. If there is a means to steal, then it will happen. It is a virus that infects a flawed business model with gaps in internal controls.

Beep, beep, beep. The alarm went off at 6:00 a.m. It was Tuesday, December 10, 2019. I was pretty sore from the day before. I took my preworkout and gathered my thoughts. I remembered having a bad dream the night prior. I began having bad dreams often around that time. It was definitely stress-related, but my more philosophical/spiritual self took it as a sign that it was going to be a rough day. Meaning I would more than likely encounter conflict at work.

That day, I trained legs. I was wearing sweatpants when entering the post office. Approaching my desk, I looked around to try to get a feel of what was happening. People's facial expressions usually coincide with the person nearest in their proximity. Nothing really stood out during that moment. I sat my lunch box down and pulled out my postworkout supplements. After taking my vitamins, I made my way to the locker room to change out of my gym clothes.

After clocking in, I wasted no time. I started working vigorously on the empty BME equipment, rolling it to the truck bed. I saw Stacey, and she told me to make sure I removed the tags from the purple FSS carts. The tone in her voice and the knowledge that I did the same thing every day led me to believe that she was that days contender. There was no rhyme or reason people felt such an urge to argue or fight, but it was an inevitable occurrence during those times. At least nothing that I could see at that point.

After clearing the BME, I asked Stacey if she would mind asking Jim or Mike if they could run a quick broom through the dispatch area. Stacey said to me, "This is a post office!"

I didn't quite know how to respond. Confused by her response, I responded with, "No! This is a professional establishment!"

Stacey became infuriated. Thirty minutes later, I conducted my first round of parcel pickups from the front window. Stacey followed me. My stomach knotted. *Here we go.* My internal monologue was preparing my psychology. Her intention was to be hostile, and I saw the anger in her eyes.

"Why are you double-handling mail?" she asked.

I didn't respond. I had to get the parcels ready for the first truck. Stacey spoke again. "That's double-handling mail!'

She went and retrieved Jay.

"She's right," he said. "You are double-handling mail!"

Double-handling mail is when a parcel is placed in an incorrect location and moved out of that location into a different location. The manuals refer to this mostly surrounding PO boxes[3], and in this case the reference would only be applicable if the containers used to store outgoing parcels near the front window were not on the opposite side of the building. Additionally, it would require me to wait until a container was completely filled before I simply could replace the filled container with an empty one. It was inarguable that Stacey's command was wrong. I looked at Jay, and honestly, I was not sure how to respond. I never wanted to argue and obeying Stacey's order would result in a failure on my part. I looked at Stacey, and I tried to lead her in my logic.

"You want me to walk one hundred meters back and replace each one of these BME with an empty one?" I asked.

"Yes!"

"What if it's half full? Do I print a placard and dispatch it anyway?"

"No, wait until it's filled."

"What if it's not filled by the time the first truck arrives? What if its full and I'm on my lunch? How will I know when it's full? There are nine different types of mailings here. Is it quicker to walk nine hundred meters back and forth, replacing each one of these? There are four different dispatch trucks. Do I leave some behind if they are half full?"

I saw Stacey disappear in cognition, realizing how ridiculous she sounded. She snapped and persisted in her orders.

"As the sales service dispatch associate, is it my job to dispatch the mail?" I asked.

"Yes."

"Would you agree that the manner in which I do so should be at my own discretion as long as the job duties are being fulfilled?"

"As long as you're not double-handling the mail."

I threw my hands up and began walking away. "This is madness!" I voiced aloud. "Absolute insanity. Do I really have to walk through the motions in order for you to see that what you are telling me to do isn't feasible?"

Stacey followed me back to the dispatch area. "I did dispatch in Westerville!" she said.

"I don't want to hear about Westerville, Stacey!" I said.

Luke, Stacey, Louise, and a few others had all transferred from Westerville to Newark around the same time. They often shared horror stories of the terrible experiences and spoke of the lack of structure present while they worked there. I was shown pictures of the madhouse Westerville was two Christmas seasons before.

"Joel, I would work circles around you!" Stacey said.

"Is that why Westerville was the shit show you describe it to be? Don't compare your experiences with mine. It's not my fault you failed at Westerville. Now I have to deal with you guys because you all came here!"

"*You have to deal with us!*"

Jay walked over.

"You don't listen to me because I'm a woman!" said Stacey.

"No..." I replied. "I don't listen to you because you're wrong. You just brought gender into this."

Jay walked away.

After I dispatched the first truck, I clocked out for lunch, and I approached Ted. "Look, man, I can't do this with her every day. Can

I just do my job as I have been for the last four months? Do I really have to e-mail the Union rep?"

"Let me talk to her," he said.

I was sitting at Sally's desk, which is the one right outside of the lobby area. Louise was eavesdropping on everything that we were talking about. Stacey approached from the far side, and I heard this earthquake of a noise. Postal 1 Sid was rolling what we call a B BME. It's seven feet tall, four feet by six feet in width and length. If I were to make an educated guess of what he was doing, I could only guess that someone told him to carry out the orders given to me of not double-handling the mail. It was a catastrophe. Sid slammed the giant BME container into the one going on the outgoing truck. Sid cursed, "Son of a bitch!"

Stacey looked at me as I watched in shock with my mouth open. "What's wrong? You look distressed."

"Oh, nothing. I'm just watching this nightmare unfold."

"What? Watching what?"

Then I saw it—Stacey looked at Louise, and her entire demeanor changed aggressively. I stopped listening because I found out what was happening. The biggest question I had was, why is it a supervisor would feel the need to appease a T-7 lead sales and service associate?

At the end of the day, I gathered my things and turned on my Uber app. "Time to go make some money," I said to Luke. A few moments later, I received a ride request. I said my goodbyes to Luke and approached my 2018 Jeep Renegade. When I pressed the Start button, nothing happened. The engine display monitor displayed the notification that the vehicle key fob was not inside the Jeep. I looked in my lunch box where I had placed my key fob earlier, and it was missing. *Damn! I must have left it inside*, I thought. I did not want to pass up the thirty-five dollars I would make doing this Uber trip.

I ran inside, and Luke had turned the lights off, preparing to head home. Walking to my desk, I looked on the top of the dispatch desk, on the floor underneath the dispatch desk, and all around. I searched Sally's desk, the window lobby area, and found nothing. I ran back to the front and Luke screamed, "*Whoaaa!*"

"I'm sorry, man! Did I scare you?"

"You scared the bajebus out of me."

"I can't find my keys."

Luke and I searched one more time, and then he took me home. I climbed through my window and started my truck to ensure the battery carried enough charge to be able to start. I hadn't driven it in a few weeks. After letting my truck run, I went to bed, knowing the next day would be dreadful.

CHAPTER 14

Missing Keys and OIG Phone Call

I pulled into the Newark parking lot. I sat there for a minute, mentally preparing myself. I was an hour early because I wanted to give myself time to look for the missing keys. I considered maybe someone had seen them from the morning group of clerks and I would be notified by one of them when I entered. That was wishful thinking. I approached the key pad of our code-enabled door: 1969. The red button flashed, meaning it was an incorrect code. I tried again. 1-9-6-9. Again, the red button flashed. I thought to myself, *What is going on?* I entered using the swinging doors and approached the supervisor's desk.

"Has anyone seen my car keys?" I asked.

Stacey replied, "Did you dispatch them?"

The comment was premeditated and thoughtless. I walked away.

Tim was eating his lunch, and I asked him, "Tim, did you guys by chance see my car keys?"

"No, I haven't seen them," he said. I couldn't tell if he was lying or not.

Jay walked in the break room. "The new code is 1974," he said.

"Jay, has anyone has seen my car keys?" I asked.

"Not that I'm aware of…"

I become increasingly frustrated. I felt like they had been taken and I was being provoked. I had lost the support of management after the visit to the POOM, and now I was fighting both sides in the busiest time of the year. I thought to myself, *OK, Joel, just keep cool.* With Tim still on his phone in the break room, I called the Jeep dealership.

"Hi, my name is Joel Benner, and I lost my key fob. I didn't receive a spare when I bought my Jeep. Do you guys have the spare?"

"No, sir," said the associate. "Key fobs are programmed to your vehicle. You can purchase a replacement."

"Okay, and how much will that be and how long will it take?"

"Three hundred twenty-five dollars. After we order them, they usually arrive in ten business days."

"*Three hundred twenty-five dollars?*"

I voiced the number out loud more so for the reason of Tim being able to hear me rather than my shock of the price. That amount of money would definitely be hard on the wallet, especially since Christmas was soon approaching. "All right, thank you." I hung up.

I looked at the clock, and it read 9:25 a.m. I had thirty-five minutes until I began my shift. My frustration steadily began to increase. I thought, *They are here. Someone is trying to get to me. I am not paying for a new key fob.*

Stacey walked in. "Are you sure you didn't dispatch them?"

The comment enraged me. "Why would I dispatch my car keys, Stacey? *How could they even get to an empty equipment container?*"

"Okay, okay, I should have just left you alone."

Walking out to the workroom floor, I heard a jingling. Sam was jingling his keys. The ringing echoed through the workroom floor. I approached the dispatch desk, getting on my hands and knees. I had hoped my phone call maybe would have resulted in someone thinking, *Okay, enough is enough. Let's put the keys back.* They were not there. I approached the supervisor desk. Ted was sitting there working.

"Ted, do you have the processing plant's number?" I asked.

Ted called the plant and informed them that my keys were missing. They said they would look and give a call back if they were found.

I was out of time. I had to clock back in for my shift. I began transporting empty bulk mailing equipment to the trailer. Every time I reentered the building, Sam and Tim would jingle their keys. At 10:30 a.m. It occurred to me that the key to my cash drawer was on the key chain. I approached Jay.

"Jay, the key to my money drawer is on the key chain. I should probably call the office of the inspector general."

"Call them."

A few moments later, I was called to the supervisor desk. Stacey turned toward me. "The plant is on the phone."

I thought, *Yes, maybe they have found them!*

"Hello, Joel?" said the plant employee.

"Yes, this is him."

"Hi, you lost your keys, right?"

"Yes! I did."

"We didn't find any. Can you tell us what they look like so we can keep watch for them?"

I gave the description, and the woman said she would call us back if anything happened to show up. I looked over at Tim and Sam by the PASS machine, jingling their keys and laughing. I couldn't take anymore. I walked over to Sam, locking eyes on him. I rarely made eye contact with anyone. It broke his demeanor. I looked at Sam. "Hey, Sam, if you ever want to go somewhere one on one as friends, maybe to a park to just talk and hang out as friends, just let me know…"

I emphasized key words in my tone. In the USPS we have zero tolerance for violence. Knowing they were trying to provoke me into going that route, I was very careful over what I said, and if one of the females was in my general vicinity, I would move extremely cautiously. My concern is they would try to make physical contact or overexaggerate one of my movements for an aggressive or threatening gesture.

"That sounds like a threat!" said Sam.

"Why would you say such a silly thing, Sam? Two friends just meeting one on one to talk…" The words that came out of my mouth did not match my gridlock stare.

"Oh trust me, I would!"

I made sure Jay was present to witness it, and he said, "All right, I got a telecom." I walked over to Postal 1 Sid's area. "Hey, Sid, do you have the Office of Inspector General's number?"

Sid looked up the number on his computer and gave it to me. I dialed the number. The automated voice took me to a voicemail.

"Hi, this is Joel Benner calling at the Newark Ohio Post Office, and I seemed to have misplaced my keys. My keychain had the key to my cash drawer, and I wanted to make sure I reported the key missing in the event the drawer is opened and money is taken."

After I hung up, I went over to Jay. "Jay, I called the OIG and reported the key missing."

"That's fine."

I looked at Jay to see if there was any strange reaction, I thought that the combination of the key code being changed right after my keys went missing was odd. I continued working, and the custodian worker Mike approached me and said, "Show me exactly how you left yesterday." I felt like he was trying to get me out of the building so the individuals who did take them could put them in a spot making it seem as if I had simply misplaced them. I didn't care; I just wanted my car keys back. I played along.

Mike and I exited the building, and we retraced my steps from last night.

"Okay, I walked to my car like this," I said.

"Okay...then what did ya do?"

"I grabbed my lunch box and walked into the building."

Mike and I walked to the post office, looking at the ground for the keys. As we returned, I was summoned to the supervisor's desk by Jay. The maintenance man had a crowbar and some tools. He replaced my lock. I was given a new key and needed two witnesses to sign the sealing of the 3977 duplicate key envelope. Jay asked me whom I wanted my witnesses to be. I said no to AJ and decided James and the postmaster were fine.

Mike approached me. "Is there a tag on your keychain that says Unity Fitness?"

"Yes!"

"They were underneath rural route 15s desk. The morning crew said they were there this morning and weren't sure whose they were."

"I must have dropped them there!"

Mike sensed the sarcasm, but the important thing was I got the keys back. At lunchtime, I returned my truck home and drove my Jeep back to work.

CHAPTER 15

The Busiest Day of the Year

Monday, December 16, 2019, would be a day to put it all to the test. All the hype. All the doubt. Everything came down to this moment, the busiest day of the year. I had been told for months, "Just wait, you'll see," etc. I hated when people compared themselves with me. I always preach, "Compare yourself to the person you were yesterday."

I pulled in the parking lot; I felt my adrenaline beginning to fire. I'd carbed up the night before, and I was a man on a mission. I thought to myself, *Let's do this!* So much determination exuded from my sense of self.

I approached the steps that led to the loading dock area. I could see it—the mass pile of UPS bags. The UPS worker had already arrived, and Bernie assisted her in loading the bags into random bulk mailing equipment containers. They were still in the bags, though. I discovered the likelihood of clerks scanning the UPS parcels was higher if they didn't have to dump the parcel-loaded bags immediately upon UPS arrival; it was not typically performed within the USPS. I incorporated the practice as routine in my duties.

I entered through the swinging doors, and it was the most chaotic I had ever witnessed. Walking in, I noticed our awesome carriers determined and motivated. I felt so much pride toward them. My energy doubled, and I was shaking. We were going to do this! We would be 100 percent on the busiest day of the year. Nothing was going to stop the Newark Post Office. The mail must go through!

I approached the clock unit and waited. (In the postal service, our time on the clock is measured by one hundred ticks instead of sixty minutes.) The unit read "0995." Like an Olympic sprinter, I waited and prepared.

Tim approached me. "Joel! Joel!"

He seemed upbeat that particular day, but I always found his moods were opposite of the condition of the environment. If the post office was neat and orderly, then he would be annoyed. If it was a disaster, he would be chipper.

"Tim… Morning…"

"Okay, three clicks to go. Hey, Sam called off…"

I didn't reply after that. I stood focused watching the time: 09.99. Those forty-five seconds were the longest forty-five seconds I had ever waited.

At 10:00, I swiped my key badge and headed toward the purple FSS carts. I grabed the first two nearest to me. My pace was just fast enough where I wasn't running. Approaching the swinging doors, I looked to my left and to my right to make sure I wouldn't hit anyone, then I went through the swinging doors to the lift that elevates to the truck bed surface. The ascend to the bed of the truck was five seconds long. As the lift rose, I gazed to the motor pool gazing upon carriers, who were loading the outgoing mail in the back of their postal vehicles. Christmas presents, Christmas cards—such a rewarding job that holds paramount value to our country.

After placing the first FSS carts in the truck, I exited and set my sights on the UPS parcels that lay scattered across the loading dock. It took me forty-five minutes to dump bags and stage parcels near the PASS machine. I returned to the purple FSS carts that remained and was able to get all of them loaded. Then I heard, "Joel to the window, to put your drawer in! Joel to the window to put your drawer in!"

I still had so much to do. The first truck from the plant arrived between 2:30 and 3:00 p.m., bringing with him parcels to be scanned and taking with him the ones that were ready to be processed at the plant. It was around 11:30 a.m. We had three window clerks working, but at this rate, I never would make it. I looked at Postal 1 Sid.

His replies were the same. "Dammit!" Sid had that blue-collar work ethic that seems to have dissipated over the decades.

I would always joke with him and say, "We're the last of a dying breed, Sid." He would laugh because I'm a millennial and he's a baby boomer.

After fifteen seconds, Louise hit the double ring. One ring means the window clerk who is scanning parcels or working on sorting UBBM is to come assist customers; two rings meant that a supervisor is needed at the front window. I already knew what this was about. The supervisors submitted to whatever the T-7 wanted. It made no sense to me again; the T-7 falls under the union and is a contractual employee. It just wasn't one of the supervisors, but all of them did except for Ted. That's why I recommended Ted be a good candidate for replacing Jay in the event he was removed. They obeyed without question despite the situation.

Seconds later, I saw Stacey walking toward me. I had no doubt if I ceased dispatch duties that the risk of delaying the mail was prevalent.

"*Joel!*" called Stacey.

I thought to myself, *Keep going, just get a few more things done.* I looked at Stacey with much anxiety. I walked through the swinging bumper doors and began jacking up a skid of wrapped plastic tubs. I saw her in the Plexiglas windows come through the first of two swinging doors. I rolled the skid of plastic tubs to the lift and hit the Elevate button. The hydrolysis noise hummed, and Stacey reached the second door. I began to ascend. She shouted to be heard over the noise.

"*Joel!*"

I continued to load the tubs.

"Joel, I need you to put your drawer in. We got a line out the door!"

I stopped what I was doing and went to the vault where all the cash drawers were stored. As I approached the lobby, Louise pointed at the computer unit next to her, Unit 3. Louise was furious.

"Right there!" she said.

She put me right where she wanted me. It took seven minutes to clear the line. Once cleared, I waited a few seconds to see if the other window clerks would walk out behind me to conduct busy work as they had been doing all week. They stayed in the lobby, and after a few seconds, I carried on with preparing for the early truck from the plant.

The early truck driver was contracted through the USPS for seasonal work. His accent suggested he was from Trinidad. We had been formalized with each other for a couple of weeks at that point in time.

"Joel, what's up, my man!" said the truck driver. "What you got for me today?"

"Three gay lords, two cages, and a hamper."

"Okay, I bring in what I got then I take dees."

Ring.

I thought to myself, *I swear it's like every time I have to dispatch a truck, the bell rings.* I looked at Luke.

"What do you want me to do, man? We have to get these dispatched."

Luke put down his phone. "She is the T-7. You are required..."

I stopped listening and made my way up to the lobby; we cleared the line in five minutes. I returned to the dispatch area as the truck driver was unloading the last of the incoming parcels that arrived on the first truck.

After he departed for the plant, I clocked out for lunch. I had been spending the first fifteen minutes of my one-hour lunch eating, and for the remainder of the time, I scanned parcels. It was the only way the post office stood a chance at being 100 percent on the busiest day of the year.

I scanned ferociously, keeping watch on the clock for my time remaining before I had to be back on the clock. Thirty minutes, twenty-five minutes, twenty minutes. I was able to make a dent in the amount of parcels that were staged. I clocked back in.

Ring.

Oh my god! The challenge for me was controlling my temper. Customers can feel when someone is angry or frustrated. I inhaled deeply, controlling my breathing. I went to my assigned unit and logged in.

"I can help whoever is next," I said.

A woman entered whom I had helped a few days prior. I remembered her specifically because she wasn't from the Newark area. She had moved here from out of state and had a Southern accent, more of a Victorian ring to it.

"Hello again! Oh, I left you the nicest compliment on the survey from the last time I was here."

"Oh, really?" I spoke loudly and looked at Louise. She smiled with rage-filled eyes.

The customer continued, "Oh yes, I said you were informative. I said you were well-dressed. I do hope you'll receive it!"

I smiled at the customer and replied, "Well, if I do, it will be the first one I'll receive since starting at the USPS!"

The customer's face lit up.

"Oh, really?"

I looked over at Louise, who was madder than a wet hen.

After clearing the line, I rushed back to the dispatch area. Sid was sorting outgoing parcels. The second dispatch truck was scheduled to come at 3:40. Midday had arrived (midday parcels are the parcels from our smaller sister station located in our neighboring town of Heath, Ohio), and they needed to be sorted. I was always remained condesend of time. It was a race. My only competition was the clock. I threw with much intensity. The trailer to the 3:40 truck was full, mostly of bulk mailing equipment. I began staging the outgoing parcels in a line, on the dock. There were loads upon loads.

The 4:30 truck arrived about twenty minutes early; I hurried as there was still much to do. Sid was getting the Postal 1 items prepared. I frantically loaded parcels into USPS disposable boxes. Once one was full, I would wheel them out with a pallet jack. The 4:30 truck was filled by its dispatch time.

Ring.

I looked at Luke furiously.

"Joel, you stay here and keep going!" he said.

At 5:00 p.m., I located a scanner and Arrow key to do the end-of-day box scans. After returning, my next stop was the retail window area to do my closeout and gather all remaining parcels and letters. Once completing my end of day closeout, I headed back to the dispatch area. Sid was there, sorting parcels into bulk mailing containers.

"They ain't broke me yet!" said Sid.

I laughed out loud. Container after container, Sid and I tag-teamed the nonstop flow of parcels the carriers were bringing back from their routes. At 6:30 p.m., the final truck arrived and offloaded several skids of parcels from the plant.

The truck driver staged the parcels with the others. Sid went over to the PASS machine and began scanning the mass amount of parcels due the following day. I continued sorting. At 6:45 p.m., the final truck was loaded from front to back. Every truck that came to the Newark Post Office was completely filled. It showed me the maximum volume of our station and was a solid indicator of what we were capable of.

At 7:00 p.m., I ate my final meal for the day. Knowing I had to finish the dispatch duties, there wasn't much time to spare. I gathered the plastic tubs and plastic-wrapped them and staged them outside. I did my final parcel select scans and filled out the truck equipment log. Sid finished the parcels and went home. All that stood in the way between 100 percent completion and failure was eight skids of every door direct mail, or Red Plums.

I removed the blue sales service and associate polo that I had put on for retail operations, located the pallet jack, and rushed outside to the first one. The skids weighed between seven hundred and one thousand pounds apiece. I lined all skids in a row inside the building.

The time was 7:30 p.m. Two hours remained until my ten-hour shift was complete. I could feel the sweat starting to seep through my shirt. Halfway through the first skid, I looked at the clock. *Seven forty-five. Okay, I'm making good time.* I took a few forceful steps to get the 700-pound skid of advertisement mail going again. I began stopping when I was within ten feet of the case. The weight of the skid pushed me forward, but I was able to get it to a halt.

At the drop, the final red plum, the clock read 9:45 p.m. I could not believe it. We had actually pulled it off. One hundred percent completion on the busiest day of the year. I looked at Luke and Luke said, "Good job." I went home and made a post on social media celebrating the magnitude of our accomplishment.

Joel Benner, Facebook post, 12/16/2019

Today I am proud to be a postman. Through unwavering determination and steadfast effort, the employees of the Newark Post Office took on the busiest day of the year. At 9:45 p.m., the last Red Plum was dropped. One hundred percent work completed for the next day, something that has never been achieved before. I am so proud to work alongside you guys. The positive attitude and pride in professionalism yield light in the future of the USPS.

CHAPTER 16

The Day I Would Put An End to the Shenanigans

December 18, 2019, was really the day transparency began to show through personalities. It was disheartening because of what we accomplished was awesome. I didn't understand why there wasn't a sense of pride within the clerks or the supervisors. To be 100 percent on the busiest day of the year with everyone still maintaining their regular days off, it was unheard of in the post office. I asked myself, Could it be that the volume was less this year There were the same amount of trucks dispatched last year as there was in the years prior. All outgoing trucks were filled front to back.

Walking in the office, I could feel the loathing among my peers. Not all of them—Bernie and Alaina were relatively neutral through it all. I always seek to understand situations instead of taking someone's actions toward myself personally. I go through a list in my head behind what could be causing grief. Much of social talk in a workplace is gossip. Speaking ill about someone who is not present. Knowing full well anything distasteful that they say will likely come back to them. Experience has taught me to never talk about people behind their backs unless it is positive. This is general wisdom; however, it makes it difficult to be social past a level of politeness because the topic of conversations every day were about someone else negatively.

Occasionally, I joked with Jay about Sid, our Postal 1, becoming geriatric, but it came from a source of innocence. It would be like Sid joking with Jay about me being young and brash. No one in our office had any idea of what all occurred the past six months at our place of employment as far as my documenting and visit with the POOM. It is information that is highly dependent on details and specificity.

A problem with government jobs in my opinion is that anyone who comes to authority with information that would be considered as "blowing the whistle" will usually be dismissed if there was some type of discrepancy surrounding the information. Meaning, is this person angry at management, and are their motives revenge-based? Often, the information is dismissed and no investigation will occur.

The problem with that is, it teaches the offender that the chances of undetected wrongdoing is increased with inflicting malevolence on employees with clean hands. Not only does this behavior put extreme amount of stress on the receiving person but it also encourages them to take part in dishonest acts with the hope that the target is removed from their backs. I have maintained this target by immediate interference if it goes to someone else. A third-party bystander can easily stop abuse on anyone if the person's motives are genuine. The three clerks that have started at Newark after myself are stellar and unscathed. The USPS needs individuals who can climb through the ranks free of scrutiny and blackmail. Ultimately, everyone who engages in dishonest actions at one point was a victim of environment. Succumbing to simply survive. The depths of knowledge, however, vary from person to person.

December 18 was probably the lowest day I had at the post office. I recently printed off an audit performed by USPS Corporate Auditing team and began studying it. Postal accounting is a different language. It is vastly complex. There are hundreds of account identifier codes, with hundreds of procedures and general ledger accounts. There are a magnitude of postal service forms that go with reporting and performance counts, etc. To look at this information for the first time and begin the cognitive work required to understand it enough to know what right looks like requires time and study. I can say it is out of reach for most people; its accounting is specialized away from the private sector. I would go so far as to say the number of people who are subject matter experts on postal accounting are next to none. Geniuses generally are recruited by the private sector who offer large salaries that topple what a government job pays. I am not a genius and became familiar with it due to circumstance not because I arbitrarily wished to learn postal accounting. It took time and study.

I believed that a unified victory over the dreaded Christmas volume would affect the belief system of the group, resulting in a bond among the work environment. The hostility and resentment doubled. I decided to approach Jay to see if he wanted me to transfer. I knocked on the door of the postmaster quarters.

"Sir, can we talk?"

"Sure."

"I wanted to see if you are wanting me to transfer."

"That's up to you. Technically, I can keep you for eighteen months. When did you make regular?"

"What we did was so amazing, but it's like people are enraged by it. I don't understand it."

"Well, it was…okay."

AJ, Luke, and Ted were in his office. They gathered there in the mornings to sit on a telecom or discuss issues pertaining to postal operations in Area 2 of the Ohio Valley District. Whatever was discussed never made it to the lower-level employees. I have worked at the Newark Post Office for six months by then and have yet to be briefed about discrepancies that need resolved. Management had never spoken to us in a group setting. The only occurrence that Jay addressed us as a group was after the verbal assault took place and I had to plead with him.

"Well, it was…okay."

I couldn't believe the words that just came out of the postmaster's mouth. He should have embraced December 16 as a mile marker in his career. Undoubtedly, it would bring him recognition and praise within Area 2.

My second week as a USPS employee, I was called over to the New Albany office located twenty minutes away to assist them for a day during their holiday season. As an assistant rural carrier and postal service employee, you are allowed to work in multiple offices. Once you become regular, then you have rights and a contract is made. I couldn't believe the disaster I witnessed there. When entering into a new environment, you do so like an infant into the world. All presumptions of wrongdoing are absent. In my mind, I could only believe the condition of the New Albany office was a result of an overwhelming amount of volume and the clerks' apprehension to resolve the issue was due to the magnitude of all the work. Innocent human responses to stressful stimuli. I have often encountered situations where the solution is so simple but it doesn't happen. A downfall of valuing expectations rather than the acceptance of the people around it—I risk appearing like a fool. In all reality, the foolish thing to do is adopt "group think" behaviors that would be dealt with administratively if discovered by authoritative figures, responsible for ensuring successful business operations. Naive in my lack of experience, I would drive on in attempt to rescue people from that fate.

My mind became blank at the postmaster's response. On a list of things I guessed he would say pertaining to December 16, 2019, "Well…it was okay" would be at the bottom of the list.

"Umm…" I said. "I guess the problems I prefer to have are the ones that were prevalent when I first came here. Newark was a disaster. I can't battle with both management and my peers."

"All I want for you is to do your job, Joel," said Jay.

AJ said, "You are just so…isolated. Why can't you get along with people?"

"If socializing comes at a cost of postal operations, do you still want me to prioritize that?" I asked.

"Why can't you do both?"

I could see AJ's point of view, but it wasn't possible. One could not peacefully co-inhabit an area with the other unless motive to work as a team existed. Without a purpose, our biological tendencies would guide our cohesion. It would revert to biology. That is the unavoidable result of placing men and woman together with no purpose outside of fulfilling the same requirements every day. It was so awful I feared for the safety of younger and more attractive (feminine traits that suggested fertility and health) women who entered the office during my employment. I avoided them like the plague. I would not speak to them. If they waved or smiled at me, I would tell them in a discreet manner to not acknowledge me. On one occasion, a new supervisor waved at me, and Thelma saw it. She immediately began texting. Later that day, Luke called her over and informed her that her performance was "rough" the first night she closed. It is psychological warfare and bullying.

I would not arbitrarily speak and perform my job duties. I believe the words that come out of my mouth should not be thrown around carelessly. The consequences of verbalizing unprocessed thoughts and emotions to people who do not have the ability or desire to filter information is dangerous. The first rule of allowing yourself to be vulnerable around someone is they must wish you well. A child will say to a parent, "I hate you!" A caring parent would never take the statement as their child literally hates them.

I exited the office forlorn.

As the hours went by in the day, I mustered up the courage to speak to Jay and ask real questions—the hard questions. I liked Jay. Part of me wanted to believe he genuinely cared for his employees. There was something warming talking to him because it seemed as if the situation would improve. It did for a few days and then went back. I could not habituate to my surroundings; it was continuous conflict surrounding fairness and entitlement. Not everyone is enlightened to the happenings of their own mind. Wisdom, enlightenment, and understanding is attained through experience and pursuit of knowledge. It's not something one is born with. If a person's life is guided by their emotions, then they probably do not know why.

"Jay, can we talk again?" I asked.

"Sure."

We walked back to his office, and I sat down. It was difficult getting the conversation going. It's uncomfortable asking a postmaster if he's engaging in illegal activities. I held up the OIG audit I had printed over the Mount Greenwood station.[4] His body language changed. I had to be very careful not to say accusations. There was no inquiry to discover if his office was being robbed.

"I guess I'm just trying to understand what is going on here."

"What do you mean?" he asked. "What are you trying to say?"

I held up a picture of the three receipts showing unit reserve transfer to the retail floor stock adding up to thousands of dollars.[5] "We do not sell this much stamp stock."[6]

F-101 Field Accounting Procedures states, "The postmaster, manager or supervisor is responsible for management of all stamp stock credits and cash credits assigned and must ensure the timely performance of all credit counts."[7]

If controls over segmented inventory are not followed, there is an increased risk of undetected theft and losses (*Handbook F-101, Field Accounting Procedures*, 13-1-2, 2016)

"I assume you are talking about her?" he said, referring to Louise.

"Is she paying you guys? I can't make accusations without proof, but it seems like she is running the show."

"I know you guys don't like each other."

"It doesn't matter if I like an individual or not. I will always do my job to the best of my ability."

"All I want is for you to do your job, Joel."

"That's all I want to do! It's the constant back and forth up to the window from the dispatch area."

"Do you know what happens if we get shopped and fail?"[8]

Shopping is a customer audit that occurs in post offices. They grade the service on a standard set of guidelines that sales and service associates are obligated to abide by. Wait time in line, asking the hazmat question, circling the tracking information on receipts, etc.

"I have no problem with working the window, but they follow me out the door and let the line build! Where are the customer surveys!"[9]

"I don't know how to please you, Joel."

"I'm going to say something to her, Jay. If you guys can't handle it, I'm going to."

"What are you saying, Joel?"

He was trying to get me to say something threatening (checks and balances).

"Look her in the eye and raise my voice one octave."

"I wouldn't recommend it."

"It changes peoples physiology, human beings will continue to do something wrong until it effects them personally, If there is no need for self-preservation, then it won't stop.

I left Jay's office. One thing that led me to believe that dishonest actions were transpiring was everyone who was guilty knew what was happening to a certain degree. Louise knew everything. It was as if Jay reported to her. Every attack was organized and planned down to what they would say to my discrepancies or concerns pertaining to postal operations. I had to center myself. It made me feel insane. No thought process was actually centered around unit adhesion or performance.

I did not see it that way. I did not want to defeat anyone. I did not see myself above anyone. I just didn't want my work ethic to provide a platform for malevolence. Everything positive anyone does is in vain if we can't turn efforts into revenue. Corruption in an organization isn't a harmless crime. It's detrimental to the people who contribute to strengthening it. The USPS is a sinking ship with the best ship crew in the world. How can we patch the holes? How can we get the cancers out?

I believe individuals have become so accustom to paying themselves that their livelihoods depend on the additional income. Doing the same job every day, I am able to see behaviors or trends that shift from normalcy. Tax return time yielded six weeks of peace, which lead me to believe that since there was no need for money, there was no need for chaos. To become moral and law abiding is to threaten their entire existence. It would destabilize their lives. These people have children; they have husbands and wives. What an absolute mess.

Giving someone additional money illegally is a death trap. It must be stopped, and we must bear through the suffering that will undoubtedly happen as a result of greed and generations of failed leadership. The ship must stay afloat.

The following day on December 19, the volume was still high but started to dwindle slightly. It was Luke's day off, and AJ would be the closing supervisor. One thing that I enjoyed about Luke was that not as many altercations occurred. On his days off, however, it was open season. AJ was the new stamp stock custodian and premature in my familiarity at the time; I knew he relied heavily on Louise for information and instruction relating to his duties.

Louise was consistent in her tactics of letting the line build and calling everyone back at the same time. It was something I really could not defend against. The sales and service dispatch associate position carried such a demand for schedule and workload that stopping and starting made it extremely difficult. It played a burden on my mental health as the continuous breaks in focus and concentration were maddening.

AJ's response to the multiple "rings" were uninvolved. He knew it was ill-intentioned but sat paralyzed. At the end of the day, I was called up to do my closeout for the evening. I began typing in my username and password.

USERNAME: YQRFMN
PASSWORD: Finnegan10222012

"The username or password you entered is incorrect."

I immediately walked away and did the end-of-day box scans. While I collected mail from the boxes, I thought to myself, *This is it. I told Jay. I'm going to say something to her.*

I mentioned earlier in this book about the challenges surrounding a co-ed work environment. What I mean by that is there is a greater chance that I would get in trouble working with females than if it were male only. I am a gentleman and becoming confrontational or argumentative with a female peer is discomforting. I believe she was trying to provoke me into losing my temper so that she could say I scare her. If multiple women say to an authoritative figure that they are intimidated by me, then what could he/she do besides act into relocating or terminating my employment? Thelma had already stated a couple of months prior I make her uncomfortable. I had to control my temper, I had to think clearly and choose diligently the words that came out of my mouth. Certainly, my coworkers could complain that I make them uncomfortable, but they must prove it. It was a gun without a bullet. I controlled the ammunition.

Walking back inside with the cart of letters, I saw Louise. I locked eyes with her, which off balanced her equilibrium. She was not used to it. It was a side of me she had not witnessed before. People interact socially and become more comfortable when they become familiar with an individual. I raised my voice one octave.

"Did you fix my computer yet?"

She swung her head at me and said "Yup!" Louise was anticipating it as I am sure Jay briefed her on the conversation we had in his office the day before.

Here is the thing about imagining a stressful situation. You cannot account for the body's response to an altercation. That is why standing up to a bully is encouraged—because the fight or flight response is discomforting. It is the body's emergency survival mechanism and will likely be avoided if possible, hence changing her physiology. Should I have had to succumb to such barbaric and unprofessional methods? Absolutely not. Its egregious.

After I shouted, I immediately became submissive, calm, and collected. Louise's adrenaline was firing, and her heart rate was pounding. She followed me into the window lobby area and counted something. Her hands were trembling. Not in a scared way but more in a "ready to rumble" way. I proceeded to call the retail system software help desk to be able to log in and do my close out for the day. Robin or Jeff entered and asked for something. Louise handed it to them, and as she brought her hand back she knocked the "Station closed" sign off the countertop on accident. One of the responses to adrenaline is it releases glucose in your bloodstream, giving you maximum energy to your muscles to be able to fight or flight.

A woman answered the phone.

I said, "Hi, this is Joel Benner over at the Newark Post Office, and I cannot get into my computer to do my closeout."

This RSS agent was a little more experienced than the ones I had been getting prior. "Okay, I'm going to switch your computer on then off again. It looks like something happened with your keyboard."

I thought to myself, *Bingo.*

"All right, Mr. Benner, go ahead and try your username and password again."

"It worked!"

"Okay, perfect, it was your keyboard."

"While I have you on the phone, I do not happen to have the Retail System Software Manual available. Maybe you can mail our office a copy?"

"I will send you a link in your e-mail."

"Even better, thank you for all your help."

As I have learned over the last eighteen months, the methods to be able to discredit, sabotage, discourage, coheres, or manipulate someone outside authoritative sources regarding someone are endless. There is always the question regarding the authenticity of an individual who may have a concern over internal controls or the integrity of the management team. A way of discrediting someone is by rendering them incompetent. Following the ending point of this book, mandatory training was assigned to our office over hazardous material and 8105s. 8105s are documents postal employees are required to fill out pertaining to transactions with money orders. Without going into information that swings away from general knowledge, the test was not a typical online training test over postal-related matter.

It required a passing score of 70 percent. If you failed, you had to retake the course. As I will state multiple times in this book, everything is routine in the postal service. When something is off, I can catch it right away. That day, everyone was taking this online training. Which is odd because no one likes to do online training. No one told me there was online training. I could not make a connection until after I took the hour-long training in between dispatch duties and handed my supervisor my certificate, saying to him, "That test was weird, man..." His reaction to the certificate was surprise and disappointment. It told me a failing outcome was expected.

So if I take factual events...

- Multiple clerks taking online training.
- Training was sporadic and followed a major event (which we will get to).

- No complaints or gripes.
- No communication or information surrounding the test.
- Test was unusual from typical postal training.

I assume everyone who took it passed; however, the group behaviors indicated secrecy.

At first, I thought, *Well, maybe this training has to be completed by today and I'm not being told because I'm not exactly the postmaster's favorite person. I'd better do it while I have a chance.*

One must piece these things together. Someone who is trying to validate their word to a higher authority will often support their information with a piece of supporting information.

For example, this dog will bite, the dog growls at strangers, or…

This person has no idea what he is talking about. He has attempted the Bank Secrecy Course multiple times when everyone else that works here passed it the first time.

Do I believe every clerk could have passed that test the first time? No way. Louise could have. Do I believe the test and integrity of this test are questionable? Yes. I do.

What would a POOM believe if someone came to him showing the data from the pass/fail ratio at offices? That the person who has failed is a moron and should not be acknowledged. However, he is a veteran. It paints a picture to him/her that is not reality.

Louise and I recently had a conversation in which I told her to be able to climb the ranks honestly beginning a career as a postal clerk is one in one hundred thousand. Even if I started at an office that was 100 percent clean, I would still face these problems at some point in my career. I could not imagine being a supervisor and transferring to a corrupted office. Most of these supervisors have families at home they must provide for. If I had a wife I had to answer to, I do not know what I would have done. Most of my free time is surrounding study, writing, and documenting. I admittedly bring these things home with me because they are problems I must solve in order to last. In order to keep my promise of walking virtuously. I am in a position where I am too old to switch careers, and years of personal development has changed my personality. What is development without credentials? Perceived insanity. A thirty-three-year-old Iraqi war veteran with PTSD would fit the mold. Are my actions selfish? Yes. However, it doesn't matter because my actions are virtuous. They are what is right.

I hung up the phone and finished the outgoing parcels to be dispatched. I had made up my mind. Tomorrow was the day I would bring it all down. I've pleaded with them. I've begged them. Nothing worked. It was time.

CHAPTER 17

Office of the Inspector General

Friday, December 20, I woke up at 6:00 a.m. My clothes were laid out the night before. Dress pants, tie, button-up shirt that was freshly pressed. I left at 7:00 a.m., giving myself plenty of time to beat traffic. At 8:00 a.m., I pulled into the Twin Rivers Drive parking lot. I secured a small three-ring binder filled with paperwork. I battled the thoughts of just leaving and forgetting the whole thing but could not back out. I thought, *This is the right thing to do. This is what you are supposed to do. You have used the appropriate chain of command. You have documented accurately and without bias. This is the next step.*

I entered the building and made my way over to the elevators. To my right was a black information board and a telephone. This information board had a list of offices with four-digit extensions.

Plant Manager. 1234
Post Office Operation Manager. 1234
Postal Inspection Service. 1234
Maintenance. 1234

I picked up the phone and dialed a number. A woman answered.

"Hello, my name is Joel Benner, and I'm trying to talk to someone that is from the Office of Inspector General."

"Okay, I'll send someone right down."

Much of what guided my decision making was centered off what I read from books. To understand something, one must become familiar with the history. How did we get here? Corruption in the postal system is not a new phenomenon. Accountability of revenue has been a battle for millennia, and there has been time periods where the organization has run surpluses and times where the organization has run deficits. I often referred to a quote by Abraham Lincoln: "There were always too many pigs for the tits." Which is a reference to Andrew Jackson's "spoils system" that institutionalized postal patronage. An ideology that rewarded postal jobs to civilians who were political supporters of whichever party that won office. As a byproduct of political victory, mass firings occurred. Postmaster General John Mclean (PMG 1823-1829) was, in my opinion, the greatest postmaster general our postal services has had to date. McLean stated, "On all the principles of fair dealing, the holder of property should be apprised of its value before he parts with it." Meaning an employee's job should be determined on the basis of his skills and not politics.

The most notable accomplishment Mclean was responsible for was increasing the post surveillance capabilities and provided a platform for the newly added Office of Instructions and Mail Depredations—the post investigative branch, later to become the Office of Inspector General. The absolute elite and upholders of integrity. They are the "Special Forces" of the USPS. An OIG agent is a crooked postmaster's worst nightmare. Intelligent, competent, and above all—honest.

A few moments later, a woman came and escorted me to the third floor. She told me to have a seat and Special Agent John Doe would be right with me. I waited for a few minutes, and a gentleman in his early thirties came in. "Hi, what can I do for you?"

Sensitive information surrounding allegations carries consequences in one way or another. It is a very unsettling topic; this is where a narrow line becomes a slippery slope.

"Is there a place where we can talk?" I asked.

"Sure, right this way."

Special Agent John Doe guided me into the OIG office area. The first thing I noticed was the disorder of their quarters. The first room had a copy machine, a trash can with garbage in it, and a couple of tables with various items on them. If I were to look into an area that I suspected flaws pertaining to integrity of internal controls, the first thing I would look for is the cleanliness of the environment.

We continued past another office and then into his office. In the background were radios on the floor charging, tactical gear, and a few certificates. He encouraged me to have a seat, and I took out my documentation. It did not feel right. I became nervous. My voice shook when I spoke. "I do not have proof, but I suspect theft is occurring within my post office."

"Which post office do you work out of?"

"Newark. I am the dispatch clerk there."

"Oh, with, um…Jay, right?"

I thought to myself, *What, are you guys buddies?*

Special Agent John Doe looked through my paperwork and read some of the text messages I had printed out between Jay and myself.

"Well, it looks like you guys have a good relationship…" he said.

I was offset by the comment. Insinuating personal feelings surrounding a matter as serious as theft and postal revenue loss insinuated my motives for concern are based off a personal vendetta. It could have been my mother. Even if I was mistaken about everything I suspect was happening, an audit or questioning was appropriate. I did not want to be right. If everything that occurred in our office occurred because of separate factors, then I could take that with a smile on my face. However, the possibility that honest employees' work ethic and industriousness toward postal operations provided a platform for malevolence haunted me. Clerks destroy offices because of corrupt leadership. Mixing DPS trays, hiding scanners, destroying equipment, working as slow as humanly possible—the Union has provided job security that makes disciplinary action exceedingly difficult.

You cannot write someone up for "working slow." You must have proof of an individual hiding a scanner. You must have proof of an individual mixing DPS mail. Every time I corrected some attempt at sabotage or dubious behavior, I did so with the motivation that our office could improve, and it has been consistently since May of 2019, but if management is committing acts of embezzlement, everything great about the Newark Post Office is not for the USPS but for the purpose of smooth sailing for the six to seven individuals committing the very acts that are driving this organization in the ground.

That I cannot ignore. It is up to the leadership team to embrace the efficiency and indulge in developing themselves personally. Training themselves, pushing themselves, becoming something that subordinates can look to inspire to. A man or woman who has transcended in a force that will impact the lives of every person they encounter. A drive toward excellence. Not to be better than the man or woman to your right but to do better for the man or woman to your right. No true leader should desire to give an order. They will act, and order will follow. Instruction and guidance to inspire people who one day will go and do the same to their subordinates. Training competent employees to be the juggernauts that will turn the tide of a 630,000-person workforce.

I said, "It does not matter if I like him or not. I like Jay! If under different circumstances, I would probably go out and have a beer with him. This is about protecting the people within our workforce and postal revenue. If the USPS goes under, it is my job!"

"Mine too…"

"I mean, do you know…like what do you think? Haven't you encountered this before?"

"I have a friend in auditing. I will call them and get some information."

"I mean, show up unexpectedly, flash your badge! Ask a few questions! Something as simple as that could stop it"!

Special Agent John Doe's partner arrived in the next room. He said, "We have a visitor…" It was time for me to leave. He walked me down to the lobby, and I made my way toward my Jeep. I started the engine and looked at the giant mail courier on a horse (that was our insignia before the postal reorganization act made it an eagle) displayed on the building. I thought to myself, *I'm done.*

Books and movies paint a picture of things that are not always reflective of reality. Confusion and interpretation fill the void of reason. We take a undeniable truth which is a 169-billion-dollar deficit and we create a best case explanation based off of factual events. We do this because it is a problem that needs solving. It is a problem that affects people, many people. In the private sector, accountability means your job. To address a possible scandal is extremely uncomfortable. Human beings tend to avoid stress if possible. Much of my knowledge base has occurred by figuring out how to preserve my integrity and venturing into the unknown for answers. I took an oath to God whether it's true or not does not matter because it's true to me. I am accountable for the things I do to a being that sees everything.

When Thelma said, "You're a rule follower, aren't you, Joel?" again, my response was, "Well, I think if a person is thinking long term, then that is the wisest choice." It's not about "getting away with it." Those are the byproducts of crime that will haunt an individual forever and give momentum to a crashing organization. The inability to do the job you were hired to do because of something happening eight years ago. The fear that a letter will be slipped under the door if feathers are ruffled. Your integrity is the most sacred thing a man or woman can possess. People will sell their souls for quick buck. That is why accountability holds paramount value to making the deterrent real enough that an honest person is not in danger of being coerced into signing the dotted line that says "I sell my soul for peace and acceptance." It will be the monkey on their backs forever, and everyone loses.

I became quiet over the next few days; we had our Christmas breakfast, and I enjoyed the holiday with my handsome boy. I kind of incorporated a sense of fatalism. Louise rang the bell. I shut off my rational mind and did whatever they wanted with no thought behind it. They could have told me to do cartwheels, and I would have obliged. I needed time to sort all the information out in my mind. It was so much to make sense of. One cannot say "It's plausible that postal workers are embezzling stamp stock" without laying the path of information that led you to that conclusion. This is terabytes of information summarized in relevant facts. We will never catch the cookie monster with his hand in the cookie jar. It is examining the crumbs that is left behind. It's painting the picture of everything around a blank canvas silhouette in the shape of what we cannot see. Thursday, December 26, 2019, I was finishing up with end-of-day dispatch duties. I had begun wearing headphones during my work shifts, trying to drown out the information and keep focus on my job, really escaping in my thoughts. Carpentry recaptured my interest. I was not sure about my future. I felt myself being directed toward woodworking. Maybe it was my subconscious mind seeking means of assurance. I believed that my faith would not lead me astray. I conceded to my feelings, trusting them.

Once completing my task, I spoke with Luke. I felt comfortable speaking with Luke freely.

"I don't know, man. The post office is corrupted through and through. I ask myself, 'Why try?' I may as well just...participate. There is no point."

After a few minutes of talk, I walked over and turned on a Joe Rogan episode on YouTube. He was discussing the new Tesla Cybertruck. It was something that carried my interest for a while. Luke walked over to me. "Joel, tomorrow, if you don't mind, grab me a couple energy drinks."

Luke outstretched his hand with a crumpled-up five-dollar bill. Being aware of what I just said, "I might as well participate," was more of me venting, but he took it in a different way.

"What do you mean? Why don't you just buy your own energy drink?"

"Because I'll be busy. Just stop by on your way tomorrow and grab me one."

"Just put it on my desk."

Luke walked away, and a few minutes later, one of our carriers came in to collect a stray kitten that was outside our post office. I finished up the parcel scans and walked over to the dispatch desk. There was the crumpled-up five-dollar bill. Looking at it sent shivers down my spine. I wanted it out of my sight. I took a 3849. We redelivered paper lying on the dispatch desk and folded it around the five-dollar bill. I did not even want to touch that money. I threw it back on Luke's desk.

"I am sorry, man. I cannot do it. I am a religious man. I will be punished."

Luke had a look of annoyance.

"Look, I believe if someone is born with talents or a skill set, whether that be work ethic, or anything, that he has a responsibility to walk virtuously. I lost everything. My gym, my family. All the good I did, my effect on people as a trainer, it did not matter. I cheated on my wife. No circumstances made it okay, and I paid for it. I had the clothes on my back. I went from having it all to having nothing. The entire time I went through this, I made every effort to try to stop it I could not. Don't you believe in God?"

I cannot recall what he said.

New Year's Eve came about, and I Ubered after I got off work. I made three hundred dollars. I drove all night. It was a good way for me to socialize and still be useful. I never could simply just go out to bars. I had to be of use. When I was in the military, I bounced at a bar called Mick's Place in Watertown, New York. I was handed fifty dollars after every shift. It was run by Mick's son, A kid named Michael Fusco. He was actually a little younger then I was. He would be in his thirties by now. Occasionally, I would meet a pretty girl.

Uber was a nice source of additional income. In between my study binges, I would do Uber. I wanted stability before I began dating or even considered it. I could not bring these issues to a spouse or girlfriend. Even now as I write this, my own dad and stepmom think that I am crazy. One cannot arbitrarily speak about this because it is so hard to believe. Putting myself in someone else's shoes, I would think the same thing.

From mid-January to beginning of March, the events of insanity tapered. Only around the beginning of March did things pick up, but I had a good idea of what was happening by that point in time. The Newark Post Office was given recognition by the Area 2 leadership for outstanding performance. Although I was not invited to attend the celebration and only found out about it by one of the carriers, I walked into Jay's office and saw the certificates on his desk. I had to fight back tears; it made me so proud of everyone. What an amazing accomplishment. During the period of peace, I indulged myself into learning carpentry. My mind was elsewhere during the workday. I did not really have to come out of my daydream and performed the same duties as I have been all year. I felt sorry for the supervisors, as they sat all day with nothing to do past their obligations, i.e., fixing timecards, occasionally dealing with customers, dealing with electronic customer complaints, answering the phone. It would be maddening for anyone. I asked them, "Why don't you guys take some college courses or something? Aren't you bored?"

The routines were the same every week. Louise would go into the women's restroom between 4:30 and 4:45 p.m. A supervisor would follow her immediately in after she exited. It was clockwork. Stacey's days were Tuesdays; AJ's were Wednesdays for a couple of weeks. Then it would change, or when there was a fight or disagreement among them, someone wouldn't get paid. After they complained or made a scene, they got compensated and they were happy. The only thing that would bring them joy was an event that occurred once a week. It happened to each one of the supervisors on different days. It was so transparent, and they obsessed over it. Really, it was like a drug. If you look at the effects of being handed cash, it floods the brain with dopamine. It was egregious. After they got their fix, they would go out and almost manically bark random duties without insight or any thought behind their commands. It transferred to carriers as unfair loops and forgotten collections were tossed on their backs. It broke my heart, and many of them looked at me like they did not want to let me down. I wish I could let them see inside my head and let them know they could never let me down. I felt so much pride in what they did every day that there was so much happening that they were unaware of. The post office ran by itself. It had gotten to a point where occasionally there would be attempts to create disorder, but I always attacked it.

I had taken dubious actions to the highest of authorities, and the only thing that resulted from it was an award ceremony; granted, it was well-deserved to the employees of Newark. There was no reason for those guilty to fear anymore and there was no reason for me to try to stop it because I already had given it my best shot. To pursue these things plays hell on my stress levels. My adrenal glands were depleted, and my personality has changed as a result of the events from May 2019 to January 2020. I needed time for my mind to heal. I found solace in my carpentry. I built my own kitchen table and started a limited liability company called "Masculente Pour Elle." *Pour Elle* means "for her." It was a furniture company. The great thing about postal work is its very routine. It requires no cognitive effort. I can learn and do other things. My first project and business launch were two tables I built over a fifteen-day period. I needed to differentiate myself from other woodworkers or furniture companies. My aim was brand building. The science behind creating a brand is through marketing. I am a jack of many trades but only a master of one. That is videography—editing. I can tell a story through video clips using effects and music. When I do this well, it can touch people on an emotional level, part of it is showing an audience the things I see inside my head that best describes a feeling I have. The arts are a doorway into another person's soul. It is a very personal thing.

Marketing my business in accordance to how I see a trade, which is creating beauty for a woman you love, is the most masculine thing a man can do. It's something she can only possess by possessing you. To be masculine for her in return for her love. To love the only thing that requires a convincing of someone else. My business launch was an experimental launch. I could not sell the tables because the craftsmanship had flaws, and really, I just wanted to get the ball rolling while I had a chance. I used 2 Denison students as actors for the marketing video. The young man presents his table to his girlfriend, and she kisses him. I found the flaws in my marketing approach.

Problems arise when someone is in something that receives thousands of views. It offsets a social hierarchy. I should not have used someone who was among peers because human beings are, by nature, resentful creatures. My concern was that it would bring about social issues that would interfere with his studies and not be taken for what it was.

The second flaw was I must take the same approach and remove myself from the equation. With emotion comes passion, from which come acts of generosity, but it also can bring out the devil in someone who has issues. I use this example often. Justin Bieber will have girls cry and faint when they see him. Why? Because his art is to be a musician, and fans are fans because they have an emotional response to his music. Take biological attractiveness with a talent, and you create desire for the opposite sex. Justin Bieber is just a man. There is nothing that is inherently mystical about him besides a developed skill that has brought him success.

Some people become so engrossed with somebody else's skill set that they create an infatuation. This is how stocking happens. When the person who has an infatuation sees that the person is just a person, it lowers their views of them in a social hierarchy, and the relationship becomes dangerous for the person on the receiving end or the artist. An obsession turns into an obsession to destroy, to expose, to exploit, or to hurt. I have lived through it before. I would rather go back to the Sunni triangle of death in Iraq then deal with a person like that again.

I removed my marketing video and went back to the drawing board, planning my next move regarding the next project I wanted to take on. I entered the Newark Post Office mid-March and heard through my headphones this laugh that was so robust and forced. It pierced the atmosphere. I looked at Luke. "Who is that?" Unaware of what just entered the building, my vacation from the insanity was over. The final puzzle piece surrounding the mystery of how the USPS became in such a daunting position. It just so happened this person was a fan.

CHAPTER 18

Do the Things I Experience
Happen by Chance?

The question that I think we have all asked ourselves is, "Do the things that I experience happen by chance?" We had three supervisors come into our office over the course of eight weeks. It was a culture shock to them. I had foreseen the challenges management would face with our office's continuous improvement. The definition of leadership is "the action of leading a group of people or an organization." The reason I was so determined to get to a point of efficiency was that it yields transparency on truth. One could say it's the Union's fault. Or maybe a supervisor could say, "People just do not want to listen, and labor will throw it out." Here is an undeniable truth about literature. There is always an answer.

> Reading is the gateway skill that makes all other
> learning possible. (Barack Obama)

The United States Postal Service is one of the most information-rich organizations in the world. There are procedures for everything from disciplinary to reward. Two things must be present for someone to read.

1. A desire to.
2. An ability to.

If you can't read, you can't lead. Period. Someone who oversees people's employment has the concrete responsibility of personal development. It is inarguable. Confidence in decisions is biased to all other factors, and that comes with the certainty that knowledge provides. A wise man would ask himself, *How is it possible such unqualified people came to power?* Ted was a very smart man, but he never had insight pertaining to events. He was kept out of the loop.

I will give you an example. Early January, I requested a performance review. Given the mass success of Christmas, I thought that would be a good time to ask. I had to tell a supervisor what form number it was—PS Form 1750 Employee and/or probationary report. The review was egregious. He gave me unsatisfactory in two out of five categories. This was his supporting evidence.

10/19-Left mail and wasn't dispatched

10/25-Left mail and wasn't dispatched

10/29-Took short lunch without management approval

10/30 Left loop mail that was suppose to be dispatched

11/01- Left mail and wasn't dispatched

11/06- Left mail and wasn't dispatched

11/07-Left mail and wasn't dispatched

11/11-Forgot to clock out

11/12-Wrapped empty equipment before sorting all mail that was suppose to be dispatched

I received a predisciplinary interview for insubordination. This was what the cover sheet looked like.

your day in court, your opportunity to discuss the issue stated above.

Q

1 On Wednesday 5-13-2020 Post Master _____ was called back to the office, Can you explain why he had to come back to Newark Post Ofice?

A DON'T REMEMBER

Q

2 Why did you not listen to Ms. _____ when she was giving you instruction? ——— WITNESS/CIT:

A CLEAN 3-M CASE, DON'T REMEMBER HER SAYING THAT

Q

3 Ms. _____ also told you you had a lunch and you still decided to eat when your lunch was over and you was not on your break. Why was you eating while still working on the clock?

A ARE YOU SURE I WAS EATING ON CLOCK / FOLLOWING SUPERVISOR
                                                          E

Q

4 Why did you run away from Ms. _____ when she tried to give you instruction that needed to be followed?

A SHE HAS HAD NO FORMAL INTRODUCTION BY MGT, WHO IS

Q

5 You told Mr. _____ to stay at work til 7PM when he was already done for the day. Why did you tell Mr. _____ to stay?

A 740-345-9534   HIGHER MGT CONTAC

Q

6 You also clocked out at 18:47 without finishing your work. Why did you not pull the 3m case as you have been instruct to do?

A 740-345-9534   HIGHER MGT CONTACT

Q

7 On Friday 5-16-2020 I _____) gave you an order to pull the 3m case prior to you leaving for the evening, why did you not follow my order and decided to clock out early and leave

A I REMEMBER PULLING 3-M CASE ON FRIDAY 5-15-20

Q

8 Do you need EAP? (1-800-EAP-4-YOU)

A NO

Q

9 Is there anything you would like to add?

A LABOR PLEASE CONTACT ME IF THIS REACHES

Q

10

Number 3. Mrs. Smith (she's married) also told you you had a lunch, and you still decided to eat when your lunch was over and you were not on your break. Why were you eating while still on the clock?

Tim the Union rep wrote down my replies.

I am not fantastic at grammar, but these correlate with someone who is in seventh grade. Why did I run from the supervisor (which we will get to)? Because power and incompetence is scary. This is not unique to the Newark Post Office only. Ten percent of the population have IQs that are 85 or less. That's one in ten. If someone would take the simple factors of smelling alcohol on Louise's breath and the intelligence of the management team, would it really be hard to believe that there is theft occurring? I have no reason to lie. It does not benefit me; it does not bring me joy.

It is so outside the realm of logical explanation that you must see it to believe it. Someone could look at this information and say, "I can't believe he's saying all this. Isn't he afraid of losing his job or getting in trouble?" There is no monster in the closet. Someone must be the one to do it. The responsibility that goes with individual job titles must go to qualified people. The future of the USPS depends largely on talented and competent people climbing the ranks. If a person is willing to accept that there is questionable actions occurring, then they must also ask, "Would it cross-pollinate to other domains of leadership?" Is there such a thing as a moral thief? Finally the most important question is, How does this happen?

The newest 204b would be the one who would complete my understanding inspiring action on my part. Not because I have any ill feelings toward her. My personal feelings toward anyone are irrelevant and do not guide my actions. I did not have a choice pertaining to writing this book. To ignore the events that will be discussed in the next chapters would be like watching a meteorite come barreling through the atmosphere and not taking cover. This book is a result of freak occurrences unfolding to the right person at the right point in time. The USPS is an entity flatlining in the emergency room with a small window for resuscitation. Do I think this mess of literature could be the shock that restarts the heart? I honestly do not care. This book was meant to preserve my own job and my own reputation. This book is meant to protect generations after me. If my great-grandfather would have encountered some form of malevolence in his youth, certainly the possibility of myself not being here would be prevalent.

Let us say that's untrue and my great-grandfather simply became bitter and resentful, developing a drinking problem. As a result, he physically abuses my grandpa, then my grandpa physically abuses my dad, and my dad physically abuses my brothers and me. I take what I have been taught parenting is and transfer it to my son. Magnitude surrounding decisions is greater than the immediate result. Events like this happen every day. Good people become statistics to life's misfortunes. I just happen to be born with personality traits that have granted me the ability to do what I am doing here. One cannot be so naïve to assume everyone can. It is simply a knack I've had since childhood. I can't weld, I can't sing, I still haven't paid my taxes, but I can remember events that occur over a length of time and formulate a conclusion that coincides with the problem at large. Does that obligate me? No. However, if I care about my future, then what choice do I have? Sometimes things happen that you are chosen for. I really have no expectations. When this is finished, I will go to work, come home, and work in my wood shop.

Not giving any more thought about the mysterious laugh, March 18, 2020, would start my learning curve once again. I proceeded to wrap plastic tubs. A few moments later, I felt a hand touch my back. "Hi! How are you?" I looked up.

"Hello…"

"I see your woodworking on Facebook!" said the woman.

In the few months I had been working on carpentry and had received some attention online, there was one individual who commented, "Joel, the things you make are beautiful."

I made the mistake of "hearting" the comment. I always try to be polite when people appreciate my extracurricular activities. You do not know who is behind a computer screen. You do not know how they interpret something, who they are, and what they will do. A lesson I will never forget.

Luke was showing the new 204B how to do certain tasks on the computer. Her name was Amanda. Luke was talking, and she had a notebook and pencil. Amanda kept looking over at me. She interrupted Luke and asked, "Can you make anything?" At first, I thought she was inquiring about me making something for her.

"Umm, well, I'm not really doing jobs for anyone," I said.

"No. I meant can you literally make anything?"

"Well, if it fits inside the realm of geometry, I am sure I could figure it out."

"Really?"

"Are you going to be working here, or…"

"No! I don't know… I am just here for training."

"Oh. Okay."

Luke was irritated, and I left. I did not want to disrupt him while he worked with his trainee. As the day continued, I kept glancing over and noticing she was staring at me. It was flattering, but I perceived it as harmless given the situation. I clocked out for lunch and approached the dispatch desk to eat my food. I could feel here gaze; every time I glanced up—there they were. Eyes on me. Again, I perceived it as harmless as her time at Newark would be temporary.

I awkwardly inched myself behind the cardboard separator that stood as a barrier between myself and the supervisor's desk. After I ate my lunch, I saw Amanda had the new Galaxy phone. I had heard good things about the camera quality. Since it was particularly slow that day, I was curious to see if the image quality was better than my iPhone 11 Pro Max. We took a picture of Luke zooming in as far as it would go to see how the quality turned out. I could not help but laugh. The carriers returned, and I performed end-of-day duties. Luke, Amanda, and I spoke before I clocked out.

"You know, I'm just quiet around here. I do not really talk to anyone that often," I said.

"Why?" Amanda asked.

"Ugh… It's just a long story. Luke is my personal overseer. That is his main job."

"Yep," said Luke.

I made the statement, but it was really meant to be humorous. Amanda may have misinterpreted it. The following day, we would continue.

"Hello again," said Amanda.

"Hi!" I replied.

"How are you?"

"I am well…"

March 18 was an odd day. Very rarely do I ever have spare time on my hands. Thursday it was back to normal. That is often how it would occur. A slow day followed by a busy day; it never made any sense. I could tell Amanda wanted to talk to me, but I was very engaged in my work. It was exceedingly difficult for me to work and talk at the same time. I am always conscious of the clock. I really did not speak too much to Amanda that day. It was just a long day. Luke didn't work with her as much either, and it concerned me because she was just sitting at the closing supervisor's desk. There was nothing for her to do. I thought, *God, that's what Jim did as well.* (Jim was the very first trainee to come and learn supervisor duties at Newark.) Amanda had spent the day making a Covid-19 update board with different colored lettering. It looked like a child had made it. I felt like I feel when my son wanted to go to the trampoline park and he was waiting on me to finish something. I went over to Luke and AJ, who were just sitting at the supervisor's desk by the PASS machine.

"So… Aren't you guys supposed to be training her?"

"She knows what she is doing."

"Well, she is just sitting there, staring at me. Luke, what do you do during the day?"

"I do a lot of things!"

"Does she know how to do customer complaint cases?"

"You don't worry about us! You worry about yourself!"

My goal was to always come in and do my job. It just never happened like that. Everything I did outside my duties was reactive. An individual could try to imagine what it would be like to work in an environment where there is corrupted leadership and ask themselves, *If I just stuck to myself, could I survive? If I just minded my own business and ignored things, would it be possible?* The answer to that is, "No, you could not." The two worlds cannot coexist. One line of thinking which is universally accepted by any business model will interfere with agendas that must be hidden for successful continuance. It's probable but not possible. It is the nature of individual behavior that was not considered. If humans were robots, certainly I could conduct dispatch duties and go home. Human beings are emotional creatures and base our decision making off feelings of well-being. Here is an example.

Let's us say person A chooses to gain his feeling of fulfillment off work performance according to how the postal manuals describe it to be.

Person B chooses to gain his well-being off benefiting through illegal activities like selling stolen stamp stock on eBay.

Person A receives a positive review from a customer survey or completes a difficult test that no one else has. Would Person B feel any negative emotion toward Person A's results as a byproduct of their choices? Idealistically, one could steal from a company and not be bothered when others work to benefit it. However, people are not robots. Negative emotion like jealousy, resentment, and bitterness will still come to a person carrying out dishonest actions.

No thief will perform acts of crime without justifying it in some way. The way of thinking transcends to something that is completely beyond realty. To say someone can do detrimental things to an organization and work hard to contribute to its success is an oxymoronic ideology. The brain will formulate biases as a defense mechanism. They will be unable to see the connection between theft and work. It will become two separate aspects in their life that are irrelevant to each other. Person B needs the post office to run to keep his job but he/she needs the continuation of dishonesty. The challenge for them is doing both. Can this really happen without others being impacted negatively?

The following day, it rained, and flooding occurred on the streets of Newark. I suggested to Jay that we start a bowling league. Jay called me in the office and showed me pictures of parcels that were in the incorrect bulk mailing equipment that I had dispatched. We started talking about fitness. The nationwide shutdown had not occurred yet, and I was training hard. Jay showed me pictures of his daughter who was a fitness guru. We talked for about an hour, and frankly, I was happy to not be around Amanda as her presence started to affect me. I had no interest in being social or building a personal relationship with her.

I think it is normal to be polite when meeting someone. The sociable acceptable thing to do after formalities is distinguish by the person's body language if that person desires further familiarity. Amanda did not pick up on my body language. It felt intrusive. Additionally, she should have been interacting with the other supervisors to learn new tasks before she went to her permanent station. This correlates with the notion that Person A and Person B can work together harmoniously without disrupting each other's worlds. As a sales and service dispatch associate, I am not able to lead. Additionally, by stating the obvious, that this 204b needs to be correctly trained over basic supervisor duties, would bring me despair.

At the end of the night, I sat down beside the time clock a few clicks until 7:00 p.m. I was scrolling through the selling wall, looking for free furniture people placed on the curb. I had started building a work bench for my wood shop and could not afford to buy new hardwood from the sawmill. I saw Amanda in my peripheral vision sitting at the supervisor's desk. Luke was at the other supervisor's desk by the PASS machine. I thought to myself, *C'mon seven (7:00 p.m.), hurry, hurry, hurry.* At 6:57 p.m., I saw her stand up and walk toward me. I could only think of one word: *Shit.*

"Joel…are you okay?" Amanda asked. "You're acting… different."

I wanted to scream. "I'm fine, I'm just not a big talker. It's not personal. I just prefer to be lost in my thoughts."

"Okay…I believe that…" Amanda appeared to be saddened by my body language and comment. I did not have any ill feelings toward her. I just didn't have anything to talk to her about. Nor was it appropriate. I appreciated her compliments on my woodworking, and I acknowledged appropriately. It should have been left at that. It was a weekend hobby and carried no relevance in my work life. One thing that I find troublesome is the reaction of peers when something receives attention. As a successful trainer, I had been in the limelight before. I have been humbled before. Pride comes before the fall. Life has taught me the measure of a man lies within who he is when the world is on his shoulders. Not when he is on top of the world. That is what people do not understand; how popular I am or my position in the public eye makes no difference. I saw the seven thousand views on Facebook as a performance measure on what I could improve on. Obviously, I appreciated the support of those who were encouraging, but to base my internal worth off that is a slippery slope at best.

When my gym was at its highest point, I bathed in my own arrogance. My ex-wife and I were arguing. Toxic arguing. I moved in with a girl who went to my gym, and my dad tried to talk some sense into me. "You have a wife and child at home, JB. You need to get rid of this girl and stop what you are doing."

"This girl is amazing, Dad. She supports me! You guys need to meet her!"

"We do not want to meet her, Joel!"

"Danielle (my ex-wife) attacked me while I was sleeping, Dad! I grabbed her wrist, and then she called the police! I have built Alpha Evolution from the ground up. I've trained 365 people with a 98 percent success rate! You guys do not care!"

"You have built a business that stands upon sticks ready to collapse at any moment."

I went back to my ex-wife a few weeks later, and a few months later, the business built upon sticks collapsed with a slew of videos released by the person I gave my credit card to to acquire the LLC along with fellow gym members. The video had thousands of views. That was the start of a downward spiral that I could not stop. Pride comes before the fall.

I had spent the weekend ripping lumber with my table saw. I always felt refreshed coming into work Monday after spending Saturday in the shop and Sunday doing chores. That Monday would officially kick off the final run of events leading to the writing of this book.

CHAPTER 19

Everyone Has a Breaking Point

I entered the Newark Post Office on March 23 at 9:30 a.m. I witnessed an atrocity. For the first time, I felt my spirit wisp away. I was so angry at what I was seeing. I thought, *Why won't this just stop? This will continue forever!* I watched Stacey sit and stare at me with anticipation. Their tax return money was gone, and it was time to pay the bills. That meant hell for me. I would not let the office go to chaos. It affected everyone.

That fighting energy I had, that juggernaut persistence of perseverance, was gone. I sat at Sid's desk, slowly preparing my placards, racing thoughts streaming through my head. At 10:45 a.m., I was able to get through to myself. I walked to the men's handicap bathroom, and I cupped my hands together and prayed out loud.

"Give me strength, give me tolerance, give me energy."

There were twenty-eight APCs (the tall carts). It was triple the amount of what is normal. I began lining them up so I could get a count. The other clerks watched. I heard the remarks: "What's he is doing?" Someone else said, "Getting them out of the way, I guess."

I had to find out how these people were stealing. The other clerks were so angry and took it out on me. Greed is the cancer that causes destruction. One must ask himself why something is happening. The absence of formal leadership should have been a warning signal. My peers found their sense of purpose by destruction and sabotage. Humans need meaning, they need importance, and they need a voice. Wrecking the post office was an expression of territory, and that is how they displayed their value. It was a message: "You better not mess with us. You better show us respect or there will be consequences."

I had no doubt the absence of structure was credited to greed. I didn't see the empty mailing equipment as a bunch of manual labor I had to do. I saw all of it as, I must figure out how dishonest actions were occurring so the clerks in which I shared employment with could be provided a sense of purpose and appreciation through their hard work. I just could not find the gap. I read F-101 and looked for it, page after page. Hour after hour. I did not know how theft was occurring. I knew it was; however, I did not know how. It was maddening. I could not hint or explain this to them. Ego is a person's worst enemy. If they could not see something, then that meant it does not exist. Ignorance can be a beautiful thing. You add ego and it becomes a hazard.

Wednesday, March 25, was the most dynamic day I will ever experience in the United States Postal Service. It takes eighty thousand words of well-structured paragraphs and relatability through human experience to implement a scope of understanding to how an organization that would be ranked forty-fourth in the world on the Fortune 500 list became a business consumed with dysfunctionality and malice. The Office of Inspector General pursues allegations of wrongdoing; however, their reports are extremely specific, around facts and data. They cannot charge a cookie monster without having undeniable proof of a cookie being stolen.

It takes a lot of time and pattern studies to catch one single cookie monster in a sea of cookie monsters. On April 30, 2019, at the House Committee on Oversight Reform, Congressman Massie addressed Chris Edwards of the Cato Institute.

"Are there things that stood out to you, things that we should be doing? Things that aren't in the report—things they need to be doing in the post office to be more competitive.'

Edwards said, "I thought it was a good report. They didn't go far enough—the crises here is much more dire here than I think a lot of people are recognizing. Those healthcare cost keep accruing every year. First-class mail keeps plunging. I would agree with the USPS that we should raise the price cap on their monopoly products, but then we should open them up to competition. You can't have one without the other. You need to protect consumers by opening the USPS to competition at the same time, giving them the flexibility. I mean the marketplace is changing dramatically Amazon is getting into deliveries it looks like down the road. We need to let USPS defend itself, and the way to do that is to privatize them, open them up, give them a pricing flexibility and let them diversify into other businesses. That is the way they can defend themselves and, quite frankly, their workers in the long run…"

"What is the most troubling part of the US Postal Services Finances to you? You started out by saying 'We have more dire consequences facing us sooner then we realize...' (https://youtu.be/-1oX-8CfiOAQ, 2019).

I cannot put words in people's mouths, but there was an elephant in the room during that committee hearing. The expression "elephant in the room" is a saying referencing something as big as an elephant can be overlooked in codified because it is embarrassing, controversial, inflammatory or dangerous. A nervous shake in someone's voice is transparent when a topic comes about that involves sensitive information. Information surrounding allegations of corruption. The magnitude of seriousness surrounding this topic is uncanny.

I have been writing this book for thirty-one days now. I keep handing off manuscripts to carriers in the event something happens to me. When there is a crime that potentially could involve millions of dollars, the consequences of released information could put a lot of people behind bars. To imagine those involved do not have contingency plans for people who blow the whistle is unrealistic. I am racing against time. From June 3, 2020, to June 17, 2020, I have been served my letter of warning for eating food on the workroom floor and a seven-day in-house suspension for going home sick early in April. The next step for termination is a fourteen-day suspension, and then I am terminated from the USPS. One of the largest rebuttals against the inability to fire someone from USPS is because it is so Unionized. I have reached out to the Unions for these administrative actions but have heard nothing back. The notion to remove a "noncompliant employee" is not as difficult as it is thought to be. To return to the statement made by Mr. Edwards, "That is the way they can defend themselves and, quite frankly, their workers in the long run..."

What happened on March 25? I saw my demise as a USPS employee. We had two new supervisors begin about the same time. One would be chosen to work at the Newark Post Office; the basis of how they were chosen correlated with personality traits that suggested agreeableness and low IQ. IQ is one of the largest factors of determining long-term life success. Someone who will easily do what they are told to do without understanding what they are doing is an ideal supervisor, for someone who relies on walls of protection for continued success of dishonest actions.

Carriers are leaps and bounds more intelligent than clerks and supervisors on average. That is an atrocity as structure should promote the value of personal development and emphasizing on individual skill sets. The contractual clerks who are above-average intelligent (like Thelma and Louise) are the ones who are running these operations (which we will get to). Intelligence has majorly affected the United States Postal Service but in a negative manner. It has become increasingly difficult to weed individuals out because they are becoming better at stealing.

Genius is hard to understand because you likely will not recognize it when you see it. People will gauge an intelligence based off credentials. There are personality idiosyncrasies that come go with genius that would make it appear as if they are the opposite. Here are factors Professor Jordan Peterson used in one of his classes that may be factors in determining IQ.

- Practical versus analytical
- Social, emotional, moral
- Multiple: linguistic, musical, logical-mathematical, spatial, body-kinesthetic, intrapersonal, interpersonal

If you view intelligence as what will move you forward successfully in the world, then IQ is relevant. When Alaina failed window training, I knew instantly there was something wrong. The response for reasoning solidified my preconception. Alaina has a heavy accent, but a conversation in English can be easily held. To send an employee away for two weeks and have them fail makes no sense. It cost the USPS time and money. It was throwing away thousands of dollars. I asked the question, if theft were, in fact, occurring, would it cross-pollinate to other domains? Absolutely. Both talent and monetarily.

Now I suspected I had entered into an environment where success is not determined by what I could do to benefit the USPS but other factors. What would someone do who wanted to advance? Of course, I considered that question and I asked myself, "Are you willing to appease the individual who is in control of your reputation and work-related opportunities whether or not it correlates with the United States Postal Service?' No, I was not because I believed that entailed immoral things. Now my options were to quit. Or fight it.

Often, a person can have an average IQ with one factor that spikes from the psychometric scale. I had the canvas; it took months to paint a picture. To act in accordance of what would move me forward in that environment was not an option. It was a roll of the dice. Success at the expense of my soul or perseverance with the risk of termination.

After preparing the dispatch area, I saw Amanda sitting by herself at the dispatch supervisor's desk. Her demeanor was authoritative, and I felt this darkness come over me. It was as if I was looking the devil in the eye. My thoughts were, *Louise! You tyrant!* It was another word, but I knew exactly what happened. Amanda was so impressionable. She had mentioned to me that she had been in rehab before. One in four women experience some type of sexual abuse in their lifetime. When trauma like that happens to little girls, it stunts the amygdala in the brain. Aspects of their personalities remains the same age through adulthood. I took the Covid 19 board she had made, the history of drug use, and the sexual promiscuity she displayed to make a reasonable assumption about her personality. Furthermore, I knew Louise would fill her head of things about me that were not reflective of reality. What did that equate to?

A woman placed in a position of power in a fully functioning post office that committed acts of theft behind the scenes. She would perceive it as her personal candyland and me as her pet to carry out whatever she wanted. Louise saw her as someone safe that she could control. Understanding the psychology of the individual without group goals and conventional structure, all that is left is what is this person going to do to entertain themselves? Louise did not grasp the fact she was destroying the lives of the people she invited to partake in crime. It's like addicting someone to a drug. A source of income that is not permanent and dependent on her willingness to provide it. She saw it as a business move. Luke is a perfect example. At one point in his career as a supervisor, he spent money radically. The source of income stopped. His finances were destroyed, and he was sued from debt collectors. Luke was unscathed until September or October; the transformations of physiology are unmistakable. When the supervisors get that fix of income, that is all they think about all day long. I started back with the paperwork the following day.

26th
February 19th – March 2nd, 2020. Incoming Management Personnel.

On March 5th 2020 The Newark Post office was recognized for its outstanding achievement and performance by the Area 2 Leadership. In the following weeks; New Supervision began the next step in their careers by learning and adapting what Newark Post office has done so they may take it to their next duty station or implementing the tried and true principles of Newarks success as new members of the employee staff. (See Attached)

If an individual is fortunate enough to come to an office that has achieved excellence, they would likely want to know what obstacles that had to be overcome to attain that honor, A few remarks that had been mentioned. "Ive Never been to an office that runs like this... Its impressive."- **JIMMY M.** . (1-21-2020) "Im not use to this." -Newest 204b-(2-24-20) It is my assumption that the path to success which I have documented in great detail would likely not be shared by the Senior Supervisors; Furthermore with a proficient staff of clerks the notion of increasing profit revenue In my opinion, would be an oxymoronic ideology. **A thorough report can be provided if requested.**

With the above information mentioned new issues have risen that pose threat to the New incoming personnel and the overall functionality of the Newark Post office. Behaviors and tactics that lack propriety. Additionally, it is my opinion the incoming personnel are confused and given the absence of conventional leadership I.E. Sound Supervision, Group talks, (What are we doing well, what can we do better) Performance evaluations, goal setting, etc. They are often bored with no clear direction or path.

From September 2019 to December 2019 I made every effort into investigating and resolving a matter that I now believe can only be mended by privatization of the USPS. I came to that conclusion after a visit with the Office of inspector General at twin rivers drive in Columbus handing over supporting documentation. No further investigation was performed. In order to avoid past issues of abuse and problematic behaviors, **(See attached)** I am recommending a solution given the circumstance.

Solution.
Given the efficiency of the Newark Clerk Craft, an opportunity arises for Senior Supervision to train new Supervisors over the basics of Supervisor duty's and task. I.E. End of day scans,

The first of the month was hell. The chaos began around the twenty-fifth through the seventh or eighth of the following month.

The following week, a new anomaly would transpire. Amanda entered in the building in the mornings, would convene with the two morning supervisors, then would sit at the closing supervisor's desk by the dispatch area. She watched me all day long. If I stood still for thirty seconds, she would say, "Joel, are you on break?"

I had battled each one of these supervisors, and I did not have it in me to do it again. The scope of purpose for their leadership entailed nothing. Mission centralized, there was no purpose outside of simply being obeyed and control. That was leadership to them. Control over what? We all had been doing the same job for nearly a year; it was the same duties every day. Our office was proficient and a well-oiled machine; for them to contribute would mean implementing some type of personal development activities for the employees, and they showed no interest in that. For someone to try to come in and throw around orders would undoubtedly impact negatively what had reached a level of proficiency.

If she wanted to make positive change, it would have had to been thought out and implemented in a conventional way to a group. The only thing Amanda knew was to carry out what she had been told.

The following days, Amanda would watch the computer screen, walk over to the section where the scanners were located, and walk back to the computer screen. She did that for hours. She looked up at me, irritated. It sent chills down my spine. *What the hell is she doing?* I thought. Carriers began to return from their routes. Then I saw it.

"Hello! How are you?" she said.

"I'm fine..." said Carrier 1.

"You missed one scan today."

"I did? Which house?"

"100 Locust Street."

"I'm sure I got that one, but okay."

"Hello! How are you?"

"I'm good, how are you?" said Carrier 2.

"You missed one scan."

"Really?"

My eyes glossed over from rage. I knew it. I cursed Jay inside my head. *What did you bring to this office, Jay? Why can't you see this coming, Jay! She is treating this office like her personal playhouse!* She acted in accordance to how the environment had been painted to her. Like there was no structure or consequences behind actions. Most people would take an opportunity like that and develop themselves or think of ways we could improve. However, Amanda saw it as an opportunity to sabotage carrier scans simply for the reason of being able to inform the carrier they missed a scan. A child playing "boss" with no concern or care of how this impacted operations. She did not understand what was happening. A completely unqualified person had landed herself in a position of power, and that was the final splash of paint on the canvas. I had six weeks until my vacation. I just had to last long enough to make it to vacation.

Amanda sabotaged scans for ten days. That was her entertainment. Luke sat at the supervisor's desk next to the PASS machine doing his closing supervisor tasks while she played boss. These sorry excuses for human beings. Absent from what was happening. They were somewhere else mentally. Their concern with what was happening was only relevant if it caused them inconvenience.

The same individuals were targeted to pick up the slack on the forgotten collection boxes or lapses in judgment. Loops were tossed on carriers' backs. It made me sick because they would do it with such a great attitude partly because they had respect for me. I often witnessed a "Go do this" command, and a carrier would look at me and frustratingly exit the building to carry out the order. They had no idea as to why these things were not taken care of or briefed to them earlier. Their energy and loyalty to the postal service yielded performance. They did not know it was from managerial negligence. It made me feel responsible for stopping the virus that plagued these "leaders'" minds. Greed—an emotion so powerful it tore families apart every day. The story was often told of siblings fighting over possessions as their parents lay breathing their final gasps of air on their death beds. I had to find it. I needed to find it. How…how were they doing it? I brought F-101 field accounting procedures with me the next day.

April 7, 2020, I entered the post office and there was nothing. No empty equipment, no FSS carts, nothing. Events from Covid-19 were about ready to produce an explosion of volume. The ordeal would buy me time as I would stay busy from start to finish. If I had seen Amanda walk toward me, I could justify walking away from her. There was not anything that she could say to me that was not designed to be argumentative or ill-centered. Her obsession was being "in charge" of me. No one saw the problematic behaviors. I believe Amanda had followed me to the Newark Post Office. Even after I displayed disgust toward her, she would still look forward to being alone with me in the building on Luke's day off. I saw it in her body language as it would change when the last carrier left leaving a short window she and I were alone together. It was unsettling to the highest degree. It would certainly be the end of me, as I knew how these things transpired. There would be a tipping point when the hope of an unprofessional relationship would disappear, but with an infatuation comes the desire to cause some relevance in the person's life. That meant hurting me. The conditions were perfect for an individual who was prone to malice to be able to act upon it. She would reign victorious at some point in time. That is how she saw it. Her will versus mine. I could tell she had played this game before. Additionally, she had received support and encouragement from Louise, who was manipulating her for her own gain.

That night, an overwhelming number of parcels had been brought in from the processing plant. Some of them were supposed to have been brought in earlier that morning. The final dispatch truck driver, Terquon (Shout-out! I told him I would give him a shout-out) said parcels had been left behind from this morning. I thought *Why?* then it hit me. Thelma had called off for three days. These were left behind and saved for her return.

Letter to O.I.G. and or Need to know Individuals. April 8, 2020.

The following information is for the sole purpose of strengthening the U.S.P.S. It is every U.S.P.S. Employees Job to report behaviors and actions that serve against the Postal Mission and threaten Postal Revenue.

On the evening of April 8th, 2020, the final dispatch truck arrived at the Newark Post office facility. The truck driver began unloading containers of mail that needed to be scanned under the P.A.S.S. machine for the following day. The truck driver unloaded 4 cages, 2 Gaylords, and 1 B. (See attached) After the Parcels were staged the truck driver came to me informing me that parcels had been left behind from earlier that day and the day before.

Upon investigation I discovered two of the Boxes were dated for the day prior. (See attached) Resulting in a Delay of Mail Violation. I believe this action was deliberate and will continue unless higher authority intervenes. When a group of people are actively engaging in illegal activity there is no longer a formal Hierarchy. Work distribution is often used as a means of checks and balances, IE, if a Supervisor who is embezzling Postal Revenue with an SSA, and that SSA calls off work after the fact, A Supervisor or Postmaster could withhold mail with the intention of distributing it upon the SSAs return. These behaviors weaken the Postal Service and put honest employee's well-being at Jeopardy.

Notes:

It is my belief that criminal activity is happening I am mandated to document and report irregularity's in events that transpire. As I stated in previous documentation, I believe it is likely that theft of Postal Revenue is occurring on a weekly basis and further investigation by Postal authorities is warranted. I believe individuals involved are now institutionalized to the lucrative benefits and have become intemperate. The lack of interest in unit cohesion and conventional Leadership shows transparency to the situation. The severity of this matter has escalated with time and will continue to do so. In my opinion, the combination of boredom and stress related hormones from hidden agendas have yielded behaviors that are destructive and break the pattern of normalcy the Newark Post office has achieved. Accountability of all anomalies must be accounted for to preserve Postal Operations. This will ensure our units continued success.

Removal from the USPS is recommended. The absence of current management will have no effect over Newark Postal Operations.

One thing that I think was never understood was by my actions were always along the lines of what needed to happen. It appeared as if I was on management's side because I would always drive on with the workload. I worked for the USPS. The moment I thought dishonest actions were occurring, I did the correct thing. Again, I worked for the USPS. Jay was extremely supportive at first. He wanted that postmaster's position so bad he could taste it. He did not consider that there is not a stopping point to growth. The office could not just stop improving when he became comfortable. It's going one way or the other. That is how human beings function. We are pack animals and go with the flow (typically).

I saw the parcels, and quite frankly, it infuriated me. Let us say that I am correct in my thinking that there is, in fact, an organized effort to commit crimes. They could never just do it in the dark. They used postal operations as a means of punishment, meaning holding mail over to a unsuspecting clerk that was on their radar. The connection that this is counterproductive to the United States Postal Services never occurred to anyone. Anytime I had brought up the issue we were in a financial crisis and the possibility was prevalent that we would not make payroll was dismissed. To me, the notion that I might not get paid because my employers could not pay me was a real threat. I had to act in accordance with that threat. I stayed over and scanned the parcels that were supposed to be scanned that day.

Friday, April 10, 2020, was the day I broke. I saw Amanda at the closing supervisor desk with that same look in her eye. I thought, *She's doing it again.* I had been getting headaches for the last two weeks nearly every day and was taking 1,000 mg of Ibuprofen. There was no hope. It was disaster after disaster, a never-ending battle to uphold Postal operations. The USPS. was falling. One must see it as if his actions mattered. I understand one man cannot make a difference, but that is due to six hundred thousand people establishing the understanding that they do not make a difference. It's true one person cannot save the USPS from demise. I had to act as if my actions counted because the truth was, they did.

"Hey, I need you to put your drawer in," said AJ.

"OK. Hey, AJ, I'm not feeling good, man. I need to go home."

"*What?* There is no going home in the army!"

I was confused by his response; maybe that is how he interpreted my work ethic. As if I was a soldier and my mission was to perform my duties every day. Maybe that is how he justified everything that had transpired, and he was simply giving me a "mission" and I didn't know any better.

"I am a human being! You guys have dehumanized me," I said.

It's true. We see the world in accordance to our own sense of self. What we find amazing or impressive relates to our own perception of ourselves in the world. Much of the insanity happened because they assumed I was not affected. How could one willfully do egregious things and sleep at night? Create a delusion that it is harmless. Twenty-eight APC carts simply to watch "a Machine" remove them. To watch this supervisor knowingly and willingly sabotage carriers was more than I could bear. I had to remove myself from the situation. I had to keep my composure; if I showed any signs of violence, I would lose my job. I almost went catatonic; it was a self-defense mechanism my mind was creating. When people snap, it is due to a pent-up amount of rage and frustration. The term "going postal" stems from postal workers losing their sanity. It was the last stand on a hilltop I knew was coming. When Alaina failed window training, I knew there would come a time where I would have to fight to preserve my reputation and my job. I had documented, I had read, and I had done everything I could do to prepare for this battle. Jay called me in the office with AJ. We had just completed a count of my drawer. I finally walked in his office.

"I want to talk about this paper, Joel," Jay said.

"Yes, sir."

"So what do you mean this post office could run without me?"

"Don't you think it could?"

"There's things I do that you don't know about, Joel. Do you know what I was doing earlier this week? I was getting mask and gloves for Covid-19. Tell me who is stealing? Are you talking about the postal service as a whole?"

"Yes, it's plagued this organization. This new 204b is dangerous. She followed me here!"

"No, Amanda was here for a few weeks before. Jim Morrison went to Blacklick, and she came here."

"No one listens to me! She's tried to offer me wood from her house. She won't stop looking at me."

"That would be no different than if I offered you wood, Joel. You have to give me something or else there is nothing I can do."

AJ said, "I think you would do better at a smaller post office."

"It's all going to crumble," I said.

"It ain't gonna crumble," said Jay. "I can promise you that."

"One person can't run the post office," said AJ.

"You're right!" I said. "One person can't. "Why don't you guys give group talks and rewards?"

"I gave you that bag and a squeeze bottle, didn't I?" Jay said.

"And two hours later, Luke wrote me an egregious performance review! I have reached my breaking point. You guys got me."

"Everyone has one," Jay said.

"I just need to go home. Don't you ever have days like that? Where you just need to go home?"

"Yes," Jay said. "Have a good day."

I went home and spent the remainder of the weekend finishing the last wood project I would do to date.

Masculente Pour Elle
April 12 · 🌐

Coming Soon. Like our Page.

You and 430 others   5 Comments   30 Shares

👍 Like   💬 Comment   ↪ Share

CHAPTER 20

Public Awareness. The Only Solution

Prices Law states that 50 percent of the work done in any organization is performed by a small number of people. Specifically, the square root of the number of employees. For example, if there are sixteen clerks present at Newark, according to Prices Law, that means four of them performed over half the work. It coincides with a terminology called the Pareto distribution.

I look at my success in two different ways: from a religious standpoint and a scientific standpoint. There is a mathematical formula that determines the odds of something you pursue turning into fruition. This is the gray area I call God's will. Ultimately, it's left to chance. With corruption in a large organization, the chances of succeeding with generally acceptable standards of conduct are reduced to .01. There are real numbers and science that factor into any given situation. I knew when I arrived at Newark, I could change the environment overtime. I took cardiovascular activity with volume and made an accurate determination that it was possible. Orderliness would become the norm. Neuroplasticity set in. If the clerks came in tomorrow and the environment was suddenly back to what it was when I first arrived, it would feel wrong to them. That's habituation. The lapse in my judgement was assuming that everyone present had the same goals as I did. Considering the consequences of something like misappropriation of postal funds—to even consider it—is so far off my scope of cognition; I did not think it was a factor. Nor is it on the radar of most people, including some of the clerks who have been working there for decades. That is the difference between fluid and crystalized IQ. Certain personality types do much better in the postal service than others, given its current state. Like Chris Edwards said, "The market is rapidly changing."

The following two weeks, I continued to read F-101 field accounting procedures. Louise often walked by me and saw that I was reading it and would giggle. On one occasion, she laughed and tapped on the cover as she passed. I sifted through general ledger accounts, various reporting procedures, and studied the Sabarnes Oxley Act; it truly was maddening. The gap just didn't reveal itself. I started listening to sentencing cases of embezzlement offenders on YouTube for therapeutic reasons. I had come up with a "best guess" of how they were doing it.

April 22, I entered the Newark Post Office. I had not seen Jay in a couple of days. The Covid-19 lockdown was in full swing, and everyone was feeling the effects. Wednesdays were particularly difficult because those were the days I would be left alone with Amanda for a short period. I began to see the transformation of temperament within her. I was getting desperate. She did not even speak with the morning supervisors at that point. She directly went to the closing supervisor's desk. I thought, *What is she going to do when I'm not looking?* Her mind was stirring. I saw the CVS medicine packages. *Oh no! She will put one of those in my car or lunch box the moment my back is turned.* I began looking for options outside of administratively. I saw Thelma, and she saw the desperation in my eyes. I had to leave work early again. The feeling of helplessness was daunting. Jay spent less and less time at the Newark Post Office, but he was there for a couple of hours that day.

I approached Jay.

"I know you're going to be mad at me, but I have to go home again," I said.

"You better go to the emergency room then!" Jay said.

"I'm sorry, I know myself and I need to remove myself from the situation."

"I've been at Columbus dealing with things. I am not a babysitter."

"How can you let this happen!"

"You act like everything's my fault, Joel!"

"Everything is your fault!"

"You have to give me something or else there is nothing I can do."

"I have to go home. I have to reset."

"Go fill out a sick slip."

I knew how I began to appear. That is when things become dangerous. Com was the way to survive. The problem was everything civil I had attempted yielded no results. There was no accountability. I questioned her on the multiple carriers missing "one" scan a day. How she perceived it was I wanted to be a supervisor because that's what supervision was to her—getting to tell someone what to do. How did I actually perceive it? Revenue loss, distortion in performance measures, emotional anguish to USPS employees, etc. This is where intelligence becomes relevant. It is the ability to see the vast effects of personal actions.

If Amanda had been held accountable and was placed in an environment where unit cohesion and group communication was priority, she would have done fine. Louise wanted nothing more than to control her and to manipulate her. Amanda saw Louise as her friend and would do anything she wanted her to. Louise would set her up to fail for her own gain because Louise cared only for Louise. Within the next week, Louise turned Amanda. Jay stayed late to oversee it, and I witnessed the same reactions I had with Stacey and Luke—blind euphoria. As if the floodgates of possibilities had been opened. Jay guaranteed protection and all was right in the universe.

I had my vacation in my sights. I wanted to build my son a swing set, but as the week before came, I knew I had to do something to resolve what I was experiencing. I could not continue this forever. Amanda had claimed she was filing harassment charges on me regardless of my refusal to acknowledge her. May 13 arrived; it was 4:50 p.m. I thought, *Two more days, you just have to get through two more days.* I eat lunch around noon and take two ten-minute breaks.

My second break was always at 4:50 p.m. where I would eat just like every day. On May 13, I began eating, and I saw in my peripheral vision Amanda was approaching. I walked outside. Amanda came barreling through the doors. I ran back inside. She started chasing me, running behind. I heard this echoing shout: *"I am your supervisor—you have to listen to me!"* The post office was flooded with carriers that had returned from their routes. The chatter and bustle ceased at the uncanny sight of a supervisor physically chasing an employee with a mouth full of food. It was insanity.

Amanda called Jay. A few minutes later, Jay arrived and pointed at me then to the door. I walked to his office tranquilly.

"Why were you eating when you were not on your lunch, Joel?" Jay put on his Covid-19 mask.

"OSHA states I get one thirty-minute lunch with two ten-minute breaks."

I saw Amanda disappear in cognition.

"How many times a day do you eat, Joel?"

"One meal at lunch, one meal at 3:00 p.m., and my final meal at 4:50 p.m. before I do the end-of-day box scans."

"Are you allowed to eat on the floor?"

"The supervisors eat on the floor every day."

"Why didn't you listen to Amanda?"

"At this time, I will not answer."

"You have to listen to her, Joel!"

"She should write me up."

"I'm gonna write you up!"

I was treading on thin ice. On paper, I appeared as an insubordinate employee. There was no defending against it. The stage was set. Fate had bestowed upon me a task. An impossible task. My options were to do it or perish. The question was how? How can I write this and have it make an impact?

Friday, May 15, I exited the Newark Post Office and drove the half mile down the road to my apartment, one of three apartments in a large house that was built in the late eighteenth century. My landlord is actually our custodian Jim's mother. She's ninety years old and had been so kind to me the last three years I lived here. I messaged my ex-wife, telling her I was on vacation and I got our silly boy a Connect 4 game. I straightened up my apartment and then pulled up an APA format in Word.

Abstract

The United States Postal Service currently suffers a 169-billion-dollar deficit. In this twelve-month report, I will highlight underlying factors that will bridge the gap to the presidentially assigned task force's recommendations that…

It did not feel right. I turned on the *Full Committee: Hearing on Financial Condition of the Postal Service*. I had a flash card note, and I began listening for the thirtieth time and writing down any new information I may have missed before.

Ms. Cigno said, "Chairman Cummings, ranking member Jordan Good, morning. I am pleased to testify in front of you today…"

I wrote down anything that I thought would be relevant for a report. My plan was to take the events that transpired, turning it into a twelve-month study that I would send to Congress.

In Fiscal Year 2018, the postal service recorded a net loss of $3.9 billion. This was the 11th consecutive net loss posted since Fiscal Year 2007 and has increased the cumulative net deficit to $62.6 billion. As part of the detailed financial analysis of the Postal Service income statements, the Commission also analyzes the net loss from operations. Net loss from operations excludes from expenses the payments for unfunded retirement benefits, and the non-cash adjustments to the Workers' Compensation liability. In Fiscal Year 2018, the postal service recorded a net loss from operations of $2.1 billion…

I needed to create a compelling argument that the postal service's financial troubles were not solely because of the unfunded retirement plan that everyone assumed it to be.

There is a plethora of complicated numbers and information that goes together. It cannot be understood by someone who would read any paper I would write, no matter how professionally written it was, and have them gain a completed picture of what is happening. I needed to find a way to present this information to an audience that would be able to grasp it. Even now when I listen to YouTube videos talking about the financial condition of the postal service, they have it wrong. Everyone is wrong or ill-informed and/or making conclusions based on incomplete information.

The question you might ask yourself is, "Why would I invest my first vacation into doing this?" Because the issues of mismanagement have impacted my life and the only way to resolve it is reaching an audience that is larger than our workforce. Job security to sharks that only care about their shark food will yield a lot of angry sharks—630,000 angry sharks that will arbitrarily destroy your life and stomp on decades of faithful service. It is a complex problem that has grown out of control, and the clock is ticking. It is projected that there is a chance we will not make payroll by September. The Gap to Solvency is public support to our new postmaster general and a broader understanding of what is happening to the public. "Nothing captures human interest more than human tragedy" (Dan Brown).

Would I prefer to have just written a paper dismissing some of the rumors and incorrect information? Absolutely. Would it have worked? Not in a million years. That left me with going back twelve months and reliving every day I had been an employee at the USPS. My decision to maintain my integrity in conjunction with capability left me with the responsibility.

May 16, I woke up and headed to my wood shop. I opened the door, and the scent of freshly planed oak filled the air. My new plunge attachment arrived for my porter cable router, and I was eager to try it. I attached the plunge piece and went to do a test run. I could not formulate a thought. I could not dive into my creativity. It was like I had never picked up a power tool in my life. I felt this force pulling me to my laptop. It said to me, "Get started." I fought it. I said to myself, *I will do a few hours of woodworking and then I will write for a few hours.* It did not work. I locked up the shop and headed to my computer. I pulled up Microsoft Word and stared at the blinking I beam. "Introduction." I could not summarize events. I had to relive them and feel my emotions. I had to put myself in hypnosis. I could talk about an event that happened at my first office with a perspective of experience or I could talk about an event that happened at my first office from the perspective I was at, at that current time. I had to bring the readers with me to show my path of understanding. It was twelve hours of reading that covered 8,760 hours.

The moment I wrote "Introduction" was the moment the clock would begin ticking. I still did not know exactly how they were doing it, but I felt it was close enough to peruse. The first 5,200 words were just familiarization of the post office. The PASS machine, how everything worked, etc. May 26, I had made it to 25,000 words. It was the best I could do in ten days. I had yet again entered uncharted territory; word got out that I was writing a book.

Chapter 21

Climax

May 26, I entered the Newark Post Office, and what I saw was both shocking and satisfying. Not in the sense that I desired chaos to prevalent in my absence but in the sense that it made me feel good that I was able to contribute as much as I did.

I walked on the loading dock and made my way to the swinging doors. I passed by one of our rural carriers, and he said, "Oh, thank God." The office looked it was in disarray. I mentioned the Pareto distribution. It wasn't only the work I could do alone. It was the impact my work had on those who were willing to work. The square root of postal clerks there. It's important to know how the impact of one carries over too many. A defeated army will begin to collapse until a mighty general barrels through to the front lines, leading a reenergized attack. That is one way I could identify the clerks who remained unscathed. When someone chooses to engage in actions that bankrupt the postal service, they do so with certain beliefs that massage their ego. To see order come and unit cohesion manifest itself goes against their self-serving belief system. "Why do you need a broom ran, it's a post office!" Jay wanted the postmaster's position. His sights did not go past that. I told him it was not sustainable. I had been gone for ten days, and the disorder had returned. "When corruption finds its way into positions of power is when a universal path to success becomes a path bombarded with wolves." Everything positive I would ever do would be trampled upon, discredited, and demeaned. The POOM had the award ceremony, and I had to e-mail him, thanking him for taking the time to show appreciation because no one told me why he was there on March 5. It appeared like I chose not to participate in the celebration. These people could have gotten away with stealing from the post office if it had not been for their egos. Does it cross-pollinate? Yes, it does. Talent and intelligence is either exploited or attacked. It would never be merited toward our industry's growth.

I looked at Sid and appeared exhausted. Sid had begun growing a goatee. I said, "I like it!" stroking my own beard.

Sid replied, "Oh, hey, Joel," Sometimes it would take him a couple of seconds to get my jokes, but it was always followed with a burst of laughter.

One time, a woman came to our office and said, "I'm here to pick up chicks" (baby chickens).

I said, "We only have guys here."

I heard Sid belly laugh a couple of seconds later.

I asked him, "How did it go last week?"

He replied, "It was busy."

The carriers were all pleased to see my return, but Jay appeared furious. I knew something was coming. It was every day. All I ever wanted to do was just do my job and have my career transpire in a natural way.

I clocked in and began tackling the momentous workload that had accumulated over the last ten days. I had filled the first truck up with empty equipment, and at 11:45 a.m., I was called in the office by Luke. I was covered in sweat and had been going at a cardiovascular pace since 10:00 a.m. There was still much to do. I was not sure why I was being called back. Luke instructed me to have a seat, and Tim, our Union rep, was there.

Luke said, "This meeting is a predisciplinary investigation interview. I am advising you the results of this interview may lead to corrective action and/or disciplinary action up to and including removal of the postal service. This meeting is an investigative interview giving you your due process of rights for the charge of failing to follow supervisor instructions. Do you know the term *due process* and its meaning?

I should have known. My walls were down, and I was happy to be back at work and felt fulfillment getting overdue things back in order. It is a terrible experience, always being in anticipation. It's no way to live. I let my emotions get the best of me at that moment.

"What is it, Luke?" I asked.

"It is your day in court," he replied.

"Got it. Okay, let's do it."

If I was smart, I should have been humbled and receptive to what they were about to tell me no matter how dubious and untimely the PDI was.

Luke said, "On May 13, 2020, Postmaster Jay was called back to the office. Can you explain why he had to come back to the Newark Post Office?"

"I don't remember, Luke. It was so long ago."

I did remember, but my ego got in the way of my senses and I gave a smart-alecky response. Luke wrote down my response.

"Mrs. Smith also told you you had a lunch and you still decided to eat when your lunch was over and you were not on your break. Why were you eating while still on the clock?" Luke asked.

"Who is Mrs. Smith, Luke? She's had no formal introduction. I don't know who that is."

"She's your boss!"

"Are you sure I was eating on the clock? I see you guys eating on the floor every day."

Again, I should have given appropriate answers and withheld in banter.

"On Friday, May 16, 2020, Mrs. Smith gave you an order to pull the 3M case prior to you leaving for the evening. Why did you not follow my order and decide to clock out early and leave?"

"*Okay, the date has to be correct!*" I looked at Tim. "I'm sorry. This is a joke. This cannot be real."

On May 15, 2020, Amanda walked out of the building to lock the trucks before I left. She assumed I was finished because I was jogging from area to area to avoid her approaching me and telling me to do something that I was proficient at doing. I had been doing the same job every day for a year. Supervision to her was getting to tell people what to do. That is what they did not understand. She exited the building; I then conducted the removal of the 3M case. When she reentered the building, she went to the supervisor desk by the PASS machine, unaware of what really transpired. She was a child eager to tattle to Jay. His priorities were filling a position with one underlying quality: the assurance this individual would not blow the lid on what had to remain a secret. It was a death sentence for me.

Luke said, "I make mistakes too, Joel! I got the wrong date, it happens. Is that what you want me to put? That this is a joke?"

"Okay, Luke. For the rest of the responses, just put 'Labor, contact me if this reaches your desk.'"

I gave Tim a friendly pat on the back and exited out of the office. I went back to work on cleaning up the ten-day mess, and now that the custodians had floors again, they began sweeping the accumulated dirt.

Louise got on the intercom. "Joel to the window to put your drawer in! Joel to the window to put your drawer in!"

So many people cycled through those units a day. It had gotten to the point where everyone was so deeply inconvenienced it became a full-time job for Louise going to extreme measures to reassure amnesty by cycling bodies in and out of the retail floor area to broaden the realm of possibility. If an audit of stamp stock ever took place, then she could easily say, "I don't know where they went. Anyone could have taken them." The biggest problem I had with that was she was willingly putting my name in question. To me, taking something that I did not earn is the most detestable thing in the world. People's lives have been destroyed due to someone taking their personal possessions. A blue-collared working man's garage cleared of his tools that he's worked his whole adult life to acquire. I imagine a seventy-three-year-old man walking outside one day to see an empty garage. He must tell his wife of forty years what has happened. The loss and hurt theft create as a byproduct of its devastating effects. To be considered a possible candidate of that egregious crime filled me with anger. It is pure cowardice to forcefully include people in one's own decisions to break the law. What choice did I have? I had to survive as long as I could. After all, it was the first of the month. Bills were due.

Amanda came in, which was strange because her days off were Monday and Tuesday. She began walking around me while I was trying to work. I felt she was being provocative, and I became cautious of my actions. I could only imagine Amanda really did send an e-mail to someone proclaiming I was harassing her, and they were in the catwalk (a catwalk area is a narrow walkway located above the workroom floor. It's a way postal inspectors can watch in discretion) watching. I always worked diligently so whenever anomalies transpired that were unusual, I was extra cautious. That means I would not joke with Sid about "chicks," referencing the joke I made earlier. I would be conscious of how I entered and exited the building, anything that could possibly be misconstrued as aggression or something unbecoming. The management staff was very transparent in their actions it became obvious when someone was around. It could have been the opposite. It could have been that they thought someone was watching. It certainly wasn't unheard of. It was tension and discomfort. I only wanted to do my job. That night, I wrote an appropriate response to the PDI.

May 26, 2020, Report on PDI

At approximately 12:00 p.m., I was summoned into the office by Supervisor Luke.

See Attached.

Luke had initiated a predisciplinary interview. The PDI was untimely and strange in nature. The first question:

On Wednesday May 13, 2020, Postmaster Jay was called back to the office. Can you explain why he was called back to the office?

OSHA mandates that employees receive one lunch and two ten-minute breaks. The Newest 204B has inquired what I was doing on several occasions during these mandated times. These times are valuable to me as they are utilized to carry on a high-energy demand position. Her approach is unprofessional and argumentative. I have become proficient at the sales and service dispatch associate position, and it is not my job to train a 204B over basic OSHA standards.

As Newark has been recently recognized as the best in Area 2 of the Ohio Valley District, I think it's fair to say that is a reflection on the clerks and amazing letter carriers. Given the repetitive nature of the job, the status of efficiency brings new challenges to management staff. How can they contribute to the increase and continual growth of the office?

The newest 204B came to the Newark Post Office knowing who I was through social media. As a hobbyist woodworker and aspiring entre-preneur, I aim to make content that is appealing to the general public. Success is dependent upon the ability to reach people on an emotional level. Ms. Weinstock had left comments on my content, "The things you make are beautiful," and shown signs of being a fan of my hobby.

When Ms. Smith began employment at Newark, I inquired if she was going to work here, and she told me she was here for training on a temporary basis. She had multiple questions about my woodworking such as "Can you make anything?" Given the feedback she had provided, I felt it was appropriate to be polite and answer her questions. I also provided Mrs. Smith with four manuals over post office operations and wanted her to do well in her career.

Being actively engaged in my SSDA duties, I noticed Ms. Smith was looking at me exces-sively, and I was uncertain pertaining why. Luke was supposed to be training her regarding supervisor duties. His response to me was, "She knows what she's doing."

Later that evening, I was waiting to clock out. Mrs. Smith approached me and said "You're acting…different."

Having a poor experience with people who become emotionally compromised, I felt this could have been the case with Ms. Smith. She has had no formal introduction or addressed the craft employees stating what she wants to do to contribute to this office, what her expectations are, what she can bring to make Newark a better facility.

I brought my concerns to management, knowing that it was likely that Ms. Smith's intentions towards me would turn hostile. The same week Ms. Smith attempted to offer me a gift of wood she had at her house, I declined. Ms. Smith began watching me everywhere I went, refusing to let me out of her sight. I brought these concerns up to management again; they were ignored. My concerns are legitimate, and although it may be inconvenient, they must be addressed. I am not obligated to engage socially with Ms. Smith, nor do I have the slightest desire to. I feel her intentions to become the closing supervisor are ill-motived. I find it invasive and disconcerting. It is up to the postmaster to use wise judgment and asses an individual's suitability for a position based on what she/he can contribute to better the USPS and no other factor. I do not wish to start documenting her behavior, as it is time consuming and will yield a zero-sum outcome. It is unlikely we will ever speak to each other. I am not on the overtime list, and my duties take up much of my shift. I want her to leave me in peace and let me do my job. I do not want to constantly be walking around her. It is distracting and uncomfortable.

Within the last month, Ms Smith has approached me nearly every time I am taking my mandated lunches and breaks, asking me what I was doing. At one point, Ms. Smith claimed she was going to send e-mails out and has threatened me with harassment despite my strong efforts to seek avoidance of her. Mrs. Smith inquired with me again on one of my ten-minute breaks, and I ran from her. Mrs. Smith chased me into the building, shouting, "*I am your supervisor!*"

Postmaster Jay was called in, and I informed him of the mandated ten-minute breaks. As a consistent and strong worker of the USPS, I will not engage in banter and argue.

Following my annual leave, I received a PDI regarding to issues with Ms. Smith as I had foreseen when I addressed my concerns with management. The PDI was incorrect, with wrong dates and order of events that transpired. It was poorly written, unprofessional, and untimely, i.e., in the midst of a chaotic morning following a holiday. I asked Luke if I could record the PDI, and he said, no, I was not allowed. I asked if he was certain. He said yes. I asked if he could show me. He said that he would.

I do the same job every day. Any contention is always reactive. I wish to do my job in peace.

I decided to cease giving the management team my documentations. With such little concern over discrepancies and concerns over internal controls, I felt the only thing I was accomplishing was making them better at what they did. When I would point out an anomaly and document it, they would find new ways to carry out individual agendas. I was teaching them how to not get caught. I gave that report to Thelma in place of Tim, the Union rep, who was off that day. Her reaction was strange. I can claim something until I am blue in the face, but when it gets written in black and white, it becomes real. Thelma read the report and disappeared in cognition. She had a blank look on her face, insinuating I was justified in my concerns.

"Now do you see it?" I asked.

"Yes, I do," she said.

"It's scary! I tried to tell Jay—no one listens to me!"

Thelma must have mentioned the validity of my concerns to Louise. Whenever arguing transpired, it was surrounding one thing: money. After Thelma clocked out at 3:00 p.m., Louise walked into the women's bathroom at 4:45 p.m. Louise exited at 4:46 p.m. At 4:47 p.m., Amanda went in the bathroom and exited at 4:48 p.m. She walked outside with a panicked look on her face. When she returned, it was blind euphoria and manic happiness, shouting and laughing with such intensity. Amanda socialized with male carriers and was noticeably less friendly with the newer younger female carriers. One had quit, and the other transferred. It was unprofessional, catty, and disgusting. I was afraid to talk to any newer female carrier as I feared what would be done to them if they were caught socializing with me. At 5:30 p.m., Louise put on her sunglasses and walked out of the building. I witnessed that sequence in excess of one hundred times since I have been at the Newark Post Office. Every time, it turns my stomach. I knew Thelma would be furious the next morning.

The following day, I was spot on. I like Thelma on a personal level. She is wise, and I can engage in deeper conversations which I gravitated toward. The dangers of talking to someone who doesn't understand what you are saying is you don't know how they will interpret your words. Thelma can understand and engage. I was able to guide her in my line of thinking, and she could put together the puzzle and take it for truth and insight. Here is an example:

"Thelma, I have a question for you," I said.

"What?"

"If you had to guess the age of the person who made that Covid-19 board, how old would you say that person is?"

"Twelve years old."

"One in four women experience some type of sexual abuse as a child, and reoccurring traumatic events stunts a child's amygdala preventing them from maturing. Aspects of their personality stay the same age."

That's what wisdom is. You take facts accumulated over time to guide yourself in the world, what is happening, why it is happening, what you should do, and what you should not do. It's the ability to think abstractly to predict problems that will come or are present. It expedites problem solving. Amanda left to her own accord was a problem. Why didn't anyone see it? Because the problems she would cause would not interfere with what their priorities were. Management's focus was surrounding one thing.

Thelma was furious, and she approached me. All supervisors watched her angrily as they were afraid Thelma would say something surrounding their operations. She didn't, but she didn't have to. To keep Thelma quiet, some type of agreement was reached. It's the dramatic change in someone that happens when they get what they want. Thelma received promise of compensation that Louise had given to Amanda the night before. I then sent Thelma this text.

Have you ever witnessed someone winning a scratch card for like $500? At 4:30 p.m. last night, there was a strange shift in energy pertaining to the closing supervisor. Slight panic followed by high energy euphoria. Just wanted to know if you thought it was strange. I wonder if her clothes will be new clothes today.

Thelma texted,

No, did somebody win 500 dollars? Lol

That told me everything was fine and part of their job was reporting to Jay anything I said to them. Amanda arrived at the Newark Post Office thirty minutes later wearing the same shirt she had on the day before. At noon Amanda, left for Park National Bank.

Friday, May 29, Louise worked on the Fridays that were her days off. Amanda arrived wearing the same shirt she had worn since Wednesday, three days in a row. I was called to put my drawer in, despite having no volume. The events that transpired cannot even be described by words. On Tuesday, June 2, I issued the final report I would make to date.

June 1, 2020, Address to Union Clerk and Associate

At 9:58 p.m., Alaina approached me and said, "Are you and Amanda okay?"

Knowing my peers have little insight pertaining to discrepancies, I said, "Why do you ask?"

Alaina replied, "She was doing everything to try and get you fired."

Seeing that Alaina was disturbed by the situation, I gave her my copy of the May 26 report I had made following an untimely PDI (See attached). This provided adequate information for the distressed PSE to understand what was happening.

Alaina continued to say, "I just don't like when people lie."

Her judgment to inform me was the correct one. I am presenting this information to the Union rep or receiving clerk(s) for the purposes of accountability and strengthening our workforce and the postal service.

It is meant to be informative and non-accusatory of any crimes. Additionally, it provides valuable information pertaining to reoccurring incidents that often take place within the work environment. My recommendation to the receiving union clerk or acting union clerk is to bring the matter at hand to accounting services to conduct a thorough audit of all philatelic products, stamp stock, and accountable paper.

If mistreatment comes to any individual as a result of this report, I will see to it proper authorities are notified and the mistreatment ceases immediately.

Friday, May 29, at approximately 12:15 p.m., I was called by the T-7 Louise to put my cash drawer in. The customer volume did not warrant the need for an additional clerk. I perceived the tone in her voice as stress-filled.

Given the lack of customer volume and dubiousness of the command, I counted the stamp stock in unit 3 or second unit from the right.

Following an accountability check, I locked the drawer and secured the key on my keychain. Given the consistency of this unit being open, I would recommend to receiving personnel that the status of the 3977 P(1) duplicate key be ensured of its seal in appropriate location.

After placing my drawer in Unit 3, I began scanning UPS parcels.

At **12:56 p.m.**, Mrs. Smith goes to the metal locker filled with stamp stock for the self-service kiosk. She then proceeded out to the self-service kiosk location in the side lobby.

At **12:59 p.m.**, she returns from the lobby, entering back on the workroom floor.

At **1:02 p.m.**, Postmaster Jay is summoned to the window by Louise.

At **1:07 p.m.**, Louise summons Mrs. Smith to the lady's changing room.

At **1:13 p.m.**, Louise clocks out and leaves, saying "Hasta la vista" on her way out.

At **1:40 p.m.**, Mrs. Smith goes outside, reenters the building, and arbitrarily greets Postal 1 Sid as he returns from his eye appointment. "Hi, Sid!"

I watched these actions unfold writing them down as they happened, playing the *Cops* theme song "Bad Boys," but neither I nor the melody was acknowledged or heard while the events happened.

As the day continued, Luke had sought confirmation from me pertaining to a comment I had made about an individual wearing the same clothes for days in a row. He said. "Hey, Joel, when you were talking about wearing the same clothes, you were talking about Amanda (Mrs. Smith), right?"

On Saturday, I had received a text message from Thelma pertaining to an individual wearing the same outfit for days in a row seeking confirmation of who I was referencing.

On Saturday, Alaina informing me of her concerns pertaining to the hostility of the new 204B fell in line with what I suspected was happening.

I do not hold the new 204B accountable because the combination of the leadership at Newark and her emotionally compromised state upon arrival would result in her being exploited for individual gain.

In my Letter of Address to the POOM, I stated:

"I live my life by a moral compass, and I will not deviate to survive. I will not watch it happen to someone else. Once I suspected that there may be problems that pose as a threat to my career, I felt the wise decision in order to protect myself was to begin reading manuals. Disorder and chaos can be restored with work ethic and persistence, abuse can be stopped with a courageous by stander. Only literature and documentation can save a soul in the midst of malevolence in the hands of the wicked. These are simply facts and are non-accusatory. When corruption finds its way into positions of power and agendas shift from a universal one (the Postal Mission) to a personal one is when a universal path to success becomes bombarded with wolves" (October 25, 2019).

Dear Peers,

I'm writing this to you today for purposes of increased information awareness within the work environment. I have brought this information to the Office of Inspector General in person, December of 2019. What you do with this knowledge is at your discretion.

AIC 247 is account overages (2).

AIC 647 is account shortages (2).

These numbers can be adjusted by $500 a day locally. The most common way to do it is through stamp stock (3). The T-7 will adjust the amount with, say, five rolls of forever stamps and twenty-two books of stamps and maybe half books of purple hearts and miscellaneous stamps that you might randomly see at the bottom of the box inside the drawer of any units on the floor.

A reason a T-7 would want to cycle so many bodies throughout the day is that it decreases the chances of an authority figure narrowing it down to her (or him) **as the criminal** responsible for aiding in the demise of the USPS. Once these adjustments are made on e1412, they can be signed off on with a "reason code." The adjustment goes to the account data mart or entry data warehouse and must be recovered.

"There is not enough tit for all the little piglets" (Abraham Lincoln).

The RSS Handbook is a "how to" book of adjusting overages and shortages. Most of the phenomena happens around the same time of the month.

I counted my stamp stock on June 1, 2020. The T-7 asked why. She said we're not accountable for the unit floor stock.

Attachment, June 2, 2020

The unit reserve custodian is accountable for all stock in the Unit Reserve (5). A LSSA may be assigned the unit reserve. However, if they are responsible for the unit reserve stock, the floor stock must be accounted for concurrently (as they happen) before any transfers can occur from the unit reserve to the floor stock (stamps in the drawers that the T-7 claimed were not accountable for).

When the retail floor stock receives a transfer from the unit reserve stock, the unit reserve stock custodian must accept the transfer in the RSS system. Failure to do so results in shortage of the retail floor stock and an overage of the unit reserve stock (6). Here are examples from Newark's RSS.

Attachment, June 2, 2020

There is a limit to how much cash can be offset a day without the notification of accounting services being notified. The ability to disburse cash illegally creates power that is reliant on an individual doing so with no repercussions if he or she decides not to.

A supervisor may decide he or she no longer wants to participate in illegal activity, but they have to watch their peers successfully gain as a byproduct of theft. Resentment and greed consumes their life, and they are unable to make insightful and accurate decisions pertaining to the postal operations. Employees suffer as a result.

Theft cannot be tolerated, and it is career destroying and life altering to the individuals who give in to temptation.

Attachment, June 2, 2020

The inquiry to discover if I was referencing the new 204B is a tactic used to disguise wrongdoing in the environment. Those who are placing "hammer to nail" when it comes to setting dishonest actions into motion have mastered the art of creating conflict between employees of a shared environment. The attention is focused elsewhere while they can act in the shadows undetected. This is the primary reason for the absence of group talks from management personnel to clerk craft.

The ability to offset 1412 can only occur with a collaborated effort between management and the T-7. It is a partnership.

Conclusion

The pursuit of this knowledge has consumed much of my time the past year. In order to orientate yourself properly in the world, you must know what is happening around you. Employees apply to the USPS with an understanding that their actions will be contribute to the organization in which they are working for. Imposing individual agendas creates hostility within the environment.

A thorough audit must be completed.

Identifying proper accountability based off information entered in the computer systems will not provide clarity in determining if illegal activities are occurring.

Every piece of philatelic paper must be laid out and counted by a OIG agent or independent auditor. I volunteered to do the audit months ago to Postmaster Jay, and my request was denied.

The accounting systems are complex and cannot be understood without study. The OIG agent I spoke to was unfamiliar with the audit procedures.

Ignorance is the primary cause of continued undetection.

The dysfunctionality in the postal system is a byproduct of Greed and access to distribute money by individuals who do not possess the credentials or professionalism to do so morally. I do not have absolute proof illegal activities are occurring but suspect they are, and audits need to be performed in order to ensure the sanctity of our postal system.

Work Cited
1. Handbook F-101 section 13-2
2. Handbook F-101 section 14-2
3. Handbook F-101 section 13-.1.3
4. OIG report FT-FM-17-016. Internal Controls Over Segmented Inventory—Mount Greenwood Station.
5. Handbook F-1 Accounting procedures.

I had laid my cards on the table. It was time to wait and watch how the other clerks would react.

CHAPTER 22

The Last Stand

I watched the clerks exit the breakroom. Management had been their complaint the moment I began employment. Now they had a reason behind the dysfunctionality. The lack of structure, absence of group talks. No communication. I brought it to their attention. The story portrayed to me twelve months ago was the Union created impossible conditions for management to be able to do their jobs. At first glance, that is the way it appeared. I witnessed Tim setting off the burglary alarm then blatantly lying about it to AJ. Sally and Sam backed his lie. The reason for that was that I had come in early to scan parcels under the PASS machine to help us get caught up. There was some type of resentment the clerks held toward management in general. Maybe they had suspected theft was occurring but didn't have the audacity to actually question it. The postal service took the hits on both ends.

At 9:30 p.m. on June 3, I received a phone call from Tim, the union rep. The blows of shock kept coming.

Phone Call by Union Rep Tim, 6/2/20

At approximately 10:00 p.m., I received a phone call by the Union representative, Tim. Tim inquired with me pertaining the letter of address I presented to the clerks. He asked what I was doing, and I told him I was about ready to go to bed. Tim continued the conversation by saying Jay had faxed him a copy of the report.

"Hey, I got a bunch of text messages saying you're accusing Louise of stealing."

I replied with "No, I can't accuse anyone of anything without proof. What I said is there needs to be an audit." Tim informed me that he had received text messages from people who were pissed off about me accusing people of stealing.

I was confused by this because if he had received the report, surely, he would have read the opening page that clearly states, "The purpose of this report is to be informative and non-accusatory of any crimes."

As the conversation continued, Tim said he had heard about a postmaster losing his job and then regaining it for sleeping with a clerk that may or may not have been the newest 204B, Amanda.

Tim informed me with the additional information that he had ten days left until retirement and I would more than likely receive a letter of warning from the PDI that took place on May 26. Tim added that I should be careful because they were probably going to come after me.

Tim, the Union representative, ended the conversation by telling me: he and the postmaster were good friends and they played golf and go way back…

Oh my god was the only thing that came to mind. I had landed myself in a lions' den with no escape. It just went from dealing with a few corrupt individuals to feeling like I was in something far deeper.

I had applied to the postal service. I took an oath of integrity upon entry. I was placed in the center of some type of criminal enterprise. *How is this possible? This cannot be happening.*

The following day, June 3, I was issued a letter of warning. The ball had begun rolling. The steps to termination are a letter of warning, seven-day suspension, fourteen-day suspension, and that was it. This isn't public knowledge; I must be the only person in the USPS with clean hands to know this information. The deeper things went, the more far-fetched they became. My decision to document was, by far, the smartest choice I ever made in my life. When you tell something to people and they don't believe you, it's like how Charlie Brown hears his teacher: "Wa wa wa." This guy's crazy. Wa wa wa. This is my life. My legacy as a man. I am a lone wolf in the biggest fight of my life to preserve my own well-being.

NEWARK POST OFFICE
OHIO VALLEY DISTRICT

 UNITED STATES
POSTAL SERVICE

June 3, 2020   low: one-per: arrw

LETTER OF WARNING

JOEL BENNER
CLERK
EMPLOYEE IN: 04790348

This official disciplinary letter of warning is being issued to you for the following reason:

IMPROPER CONDUCT

As a Postal employee, you should be well aware that you are required to follow instructions. You are also aware that you are to perform your all the designated duties of your position efficiently and effectively. However, on May 13 and 15, 2020, you failed to follow instructions given to you by management. On May 13, you were observed eating outside of your lunch break by acting Supervisor Krysta Weinstock. She instructed you to continue working as you had already had your lunch break. You ignored her, going out to the dock with your food. During your Pre-Disciplinary Interview, I asked why you were eating while working on the clock. You said, "I was going off of your guys' example."

On May 15, I instructed you to pull the 3M (Missorted, Missequenced, and Missent mail) case prior to you clocking out and leaving for the day. Afterwards, when I was locking the gates and closing the mail truck doors, I saw you leave the office. I went inside and noticed the 3M case had not been pulled. During your interview, I asked why you failed to follow my instruction. You told me your vacation started May 16 and you remembered pulling the 3M case. You also stated you knew you did pull the 3M because it was before your vacation. Management will not tolerate your failure to follow instructions.

Your actions constitute a violation of USPS Standards of Conduct as expressed in the **Employee and Labor Relations Manual (ELM)...**

Section 665.13 Discharge of Duties
Employees are expected to discharge their assigned duties conscientiously and effectively.

Section 665.15 Obedience to Orders
Employees must obey the instructions of their supervisors. If an employee has reason to question the propriety of a supervisor's order, the individual must nevertheless carry out the order and may immediately file a protest in writing to the official in charge of the installation or may appeal through official channels.

DISC   1

Stacey had given me the letter of warning. I gave her the sheet that spoke about the phone call I received from Ted.

Jay approached me. "This is all a game to you!"

"Can I see the Postal Service Form 3977 duplicate key?"

"No!"

"Can I see the Postal Service Form 3294 Cash and Stamp Count Summary?"

"No!"

"Are you stealing from this office?"

"No!"

"Do you know if anyone is?"

"*I don't know!*"

AJ said, "Louise is responsible for the retail floor stock, not me!"

"*Quiet!*" said Jay to AJ.

After the conversation ended, I approached Postal 1 Sid. "Sid, I need the Ohio Valley District Manager's e-mail and that of the Eastern Area VP." At 6:30 p.m., I went to log into my e-mail; my access was denied. I tried a different computer; my access was denied. I wanted the corruption away from me. I could not take it anymore. It was darkening. It was illegal. It was wrong. It was self-destructive. Why wouldn't anyone try to stop it? What kind of person would I be if I engaged in this? What kind of dad would I be?

I left for home, put the car in park, and laid out all my documentation. I had lived at my computer and laptop this year. I have studied hours on in. Everything was because of greed! Everything! Every delay in mail, every dubious action, every malicious attack was because of greed!

Facebook

A game? No, no. This is my *life*. I've gone to the POOM, I've gone to the Office of Inspector General, I have gone to the Union, now I'm going to the public. There needs to be a thorough and complete audit of all philatelic stock at the Newark Post Office. I do not want the corruption around me.

June 4, 2020, I entered into the Newark Post Office and went right to Jay's office. I knocked.

"I tried to send an e-mail last night," I said. "Can I send an e-mail right now?"

"No!" said Jay.

"It's regarding postal revenue. Can I send an e-mail?"

"*No!*"

Stacey and AJ followed me out. I worked for a few minutes but could not take it.

"I need to send an e-mail. AJ, can I send an e-mail?"

"No," he replied.

"You can do that on your own time," Stacey said.

"AJ, does it concern you that there is possible theft occurring?" I asked.

"Yes," he said.

"What is a Postal Form 3294, AJ? You are the stamp stock custodian, AJ!"

"Joel!" said Stacey. "There was just an audit recently done!"

"Let me see the Postal Form 3866P, AJ," I said.

"Don't answer him," Stacey said.

"*How can you account for something when you don't know how,* AJ? Can I go to Twin Rivers?"

AJ's voice shook. "No…"

"Stacey, what's section 665.13 in the Employee Labor Manual?" I asked.

"I don't know."

"Well, you should know, Stacey! You slapped it in on a sheet of paper that affects my life and handed it to me yesterday!"

"Now he's threatening us!" she said. "Whatever—let him go!"

I went to my Jeep and passed by Mike, our custodian. "I'm going to go talk to the POOM, Mike."

I made my way to Twin Rivers and dialed the POOM's number.

His secretary answered, "Bradley Grubbs's office, how may we help you?"

"Hi, I'm Joel Benner from the Newark Post Office. I need to talk to the POOM."

"Oh, he is in telecom meetings. You have to have an appointment for that."

"Can you leave him a message?"

"Sure, I can leave him a message."

"Tell him I tried to send an e-mail, but my e-mail wasn't working."

"I'll tell him you tried to send an e-mail, but they shut your e-mail down. Got it."

"I did not say *they*! I drove forty-five minutes here—can you give me the extension to OIG?" (It had been removed since my first visit.)

"It's 1800-OIG-USPS…"

I hung up the phone. I would not leave here until I spoke to someone. A woman entered from around the corner.

"Excuse me, ma'am, is Special Agent John Doe here?"

"Yes!" she said. "I just saw him. I will go get him!"

I waited for a few seconds, and two men walked out of the fire escape exit next to the elevators. They were postal inspectors.

"Oh, thank God. Is there someplace we can talk?"

"We know who you are," they said.

"You know me? Good!" I felt relief.

"Yes, we know your concerns. We—"

I interrupted them, "Is there someplace we can go and talk?"

In retrospect, I think they came down to escort me out, but I had brought my notebook with the letter of address to union clerks and associates. The postal inspectors led me to the third floor, where we sat.

"I think there is a real possibility that theft is happening at our office. Do you guys know anything about accounting? How are they doing it? Have you ever performed stamp stock audit?" I asked.

"Maybe you ought to start thinking about your job," said the postal inspector. "You can't post things on social media because you're mad at the postmaster. You have a son, right?"

"Mad at my postmaster? My feelings have nothing to do with it! I'm telling you I have a year's worth of documenting, and at the very least, an audit needs to be performed!"

"Well, OIG takes care of this stuff. Sometimes they are on cases for years."

"We don't have years! We have until September until we cannot make payroll!"

"I can see the stress in your eyes. Do you need to talk with a EAP counselor?"

"No, thank you. The audit procedures are in F-101 field accounting procedu—"

"I know F-101!"

The postal inspectors walked me down to the fire escape. I drove back to the Newark Post Office. The first thing I was told to do was put in my drawer. I did as instructed.

The POOM placed Amanda at a different office, and a woman named Val took the fifth supervisor position. She has twin boys and does a fantastic job. She was a letter carrier for eighteen years.

I was served another predisciplinary interview. I told AJ to put the same replies on all the questions: "I am aware of my three attendance issues. Moving forward, you will no longer have any issues with myself and attendance. I will abide by the attendance regulations as stated in 665.41 Requirement of Regular Attendance per Employee Labor Manual."

I had nowhere left to turn. Nowhere left to go. My fight for the United States Postal Service was over; my book was halfway completed without a solid statement of how they were able to do it. All was seemingly lost. I was walking in a twilight zone of uncertainty of what will happen tomorrow. I thought I worked for the United States Postal Service. Maybe I just wasted two years of my life. Maybe I really am a fool.

CHAPTER 23

Excludable Stamp Stock Inventory

On June 15, 2020, came salvation. "Excludable stamp stock inventory"—a category created to allow post offices to carry more saleable stamp stock during Christmas time. It was the "broken bulb" I needed to light up the entire strand of Christmas lights. Excludable stamp stock inventory bridged the gap. I had searched so deep into postal accounting that I was in outer space when the answer to it lay hidden in low earth orbit. Why had no one found this before? It was not monitorable.

Excludable stamp stock inventory is a "storage unit" postal management created to save time spent monitoring and messaging units that carried excess amount of stamp stock during Quarter 2 (Merry Christmas). Stamp fulfillment services allows three stamp stock shipments a month to occur, with the ability to bypass the third after an acknowledgment of a warning. The receipts mentioned after December 16 in this book are transfers from the unit reserve (the room that is known as the vault) of stamps to the retail floor stock (the window lobby area). At the end of the day, stamps are transferred to excludable stamp stock inventory, then stamps are virtually walked out of the building.

It is a multimillion-dollar business within a business; 12,151 offices exceeded the three stock ordering max from Stamp Fulfilment Services in 2018, and the number is rising as supervisors are taught how to be a leader in the USPS. Create disorder, manipulate the environment, create as much smoke while fulfilling a Universal Mandate of delivering 47 percent of the world's mail.

Louis DeJoy was appointed Postmaster General on June 16, 2020. Dejoy is a Brooklyn Juggernaut and will go down in history as the final Postmaster General of the United States Postal Service as we transition to a privately run postal service.

Federal employees must abide by the rules set forth by the government. That includes not engaging in political campaigns, committing acts of theft, embezzling, pilfering, and so on. The delusion that congress will waste American taxpayers' money is a preconceived notion that has sentenced us all to a fate which postal employees have bestowed upon ourselves. I take responsibility and maintain my loyalty to the United States Postal Service. This book is for the sole purpose of enlightening the public and to protect the reputation of those responsible for making the changes needed to better fulfill our obligation of carrying out a Universal Service Mandate.

9:29 ⌁   ⏹ LTE 🔋

< Carol Reichle Burkett ▶ Information
and News for Postal Employees   ...
⏺ Admin · Yesterday at 6:59 AM · 🌐

3 shares

Terry Finnerty
Good riddance. Don't let the door hit you
in the ass, on your way out!
1d Like Reply   👍😆 6

John Faraone
Like the new one will be any better !! They'll
all were terrible starting with starvin
Marvin !!
1d Like Reply   👍 1

Kathy Woods
John Faraone Carvin Marvin
1d Like Reply   👍 1

John Faraone
One in the same carved things out and
starved the carriers lol!!! Good riddance
to all of them the guy coming in is no
gem either !!
23h Like Reply   👍 1

Write a reply...

Adria Brown
She couldn't handle the pressure of this
pandemic. How convenient that she's
retiring now. Not saying this hasn't been
planned but it's ironic

It was Tuesday, so I knew it was Stacey's turn to be compensated. Stacey had such fury toward me. It's as if I was to blame for all of her troubles. At 1:00 p.m., I approached Stacey to ask her if I could wear headphones while I did dispatch. It was not as stationary as a letter case was, but I thought I would try my luck.

She said, "No, and you will put your drawer in every single day, put it in at noon. You will wear the blue polo shirt all day long whether you are on the window or not."

I went outside and googled "stamp stock spoil date USPS." There it was. Stamp Stock Accountability Report Number FT-AR-19-008 by the Office of Inspector General. The question goes back to "If there was an easy way to steal at one office, would it be happening everywhere?" I printed out the report and studied it that night.

June 17, I entered into the Newark Post Office, and I saw AJ and Stacey. I found myself feeling sad. I wanted to save them. After lunch, I approached with the report in my hand. I spoke softly. "Can I show you guys something?"

"Sure," said AJ.

"Um, it's a report that OIG made. We are going private. It's over."

"We're not going private!" Stacey said. "They have been saying that forever!"

"So in 2006, the Postal Enhancement and Accountability Act happened, and really it was a 'Get it together or Perish Act.' They wanted us to gain stronger financial footing through efficiency rather than raising our postage rates. We're out of money. September we are scheduled to not make payroll, Stacey. It's over," I said.

I was howling at the moon. They did not understand. I was Noah warning people about a flood.

I went over to the accountable cart and sat there for a moment. AJ handed me a sheet of paper.

NEWARK POST OFFICE
OHIO VALLEY DISTRICT

UNITED STATES
POSTAL SERVICE

June 16, 2020   7day-uns-att: amw

NOTICE OF SUSPENSION OF 7 DAYS

JOEL HENNER
CLERK
EMPLOYEE IN: 04790348

You are hereby notified that you will be suspended for a period of seven (7) calendar days in accordance with Article 16 of the National Agreement. However, if a timely grievance is initiated, the effective date of the suspension will be delayed until disposition of the grievance, either by settlement or an arbitrator's final and binding decision. You will at that time be advised as to the effective dates of the suspension. If you do not elect to file a grievance concerning this suspension, you will be notified of the effective dates of the suspension. The reason for the suspension is:

UNSATISFACTORY ATTENDANCE

A review of your records indicates that you have not been regular in attendance on the following dates:

DATE	HOURS	TYPE
04/10/2020	5.17	USL
04/22/2020	4.70	UPLWP
06/04/2020	2.09	USL

Your failure to maintain regular attendance constitutes a violation of USPS Standards of Conduct as expressed in the **Employee and Labor Relations Manual (ELM):**

Section 511.43 Employee Responsibilities
Employees are expected to maintain their assigned schedule and must make every effort to avoid unscheduled absences. In addition, employees must provide acceptable evidence for absences when required.

Section 665.41 Requirement of Regular Attendance
Employees are required to be regular in attendance. Failure to be regular in attendance may result in disciplinary action, including removal from the Postal Service.

DISC   1

AJ said, "This is your seven-day suspension. You have fourteen days to get with the Union and appeal against it. I just need you to sign right here."

I picked up the pen and began to sign. I was sad for AJ. AJ and I were brothers in arms. We had both fought the war on terror in Iraq in 2008.

"You know, man, I see you with your little girls, and it's heartbreaking to think of what could happen. They are being walked out and sold on eBay," I said.

The shakiness in AJ's voice returned. That wall of fear that hits them in the face and takes over their bodies. "I'm in charge of like 140,000 dollars. Trust me, I know."

That response alone took away all shadows of doubt.

After the parcels had been dispatched, I walked outside to see Luke smoking in the smoker's pit. I told him the same thing I had told AJ. When the word *eBay* came up, his eyes became wide.

"You know, Joel, I have like five backup plans. I don't know, I just want to be on a boat sailing around the world."

On June 19, the same euphoric occurrences continued. It would not stop; they could not stop. Institutionalized. It was done. Stamp Fulfillment Center. The definition of *fulfill*: "to bring to completion or reality."

Yesterday, June 23, the Union president arrived at the Newark Post Office. I took a class over the No-FEAR Act, which is the Notification and Federal Employee Antidiscrimination and Retaliation Act of 2002. It is a law set in place to discriminate managers and supervisors from participating in retaliation attacks against whistleblowers for reporting wrongdoings.

The Union president, Sarah, called me back to the break room after Jay was finished.

"Hello, Joel," she said. "How are you?"

"I'm well, thank you."

"How long have you been at Newark? Do you like it here?"

"I do like it here. Everyone is great. I enjoy the people I work with. We all work together collectively contributing to the future of the USPS."

"Well, that is good. I told Jay some of the older people are set in our ways, and it's just an age difference. We're moody and tired. You young guys are so full of energy."

I gave Sarah an earnest grin, not making eye contact.

"Well, I see here you have a seven-day suspension. Jay wanted it on your file for a year. I felt that was a bit excessive."

"There won't be any more insubordination from me. I've learned my lesson."

"I think it's just an age thing. You know what, I'll try to get this removed."

"Thank you so much."

Today, June 25, 2020, I showed Bernie the beginning of Chapter 23, speaking about the USPS going private.

Bernie said, "We can't go private! They will tear us apart!"

"Why do you think I wrote the book, Bernie? No one knows about this. Don't worry, my friend. An honest man's pillow is his peace of mind. I will finish the book tonight and write the report that goes with it this weekend. Then…I will return to my wood shop."

"Either write something worth reading or do something worth writing" (Benjamin Franklin).

I must be the man I wish my son to be.

SUMMARY

Let it go private. It's time.

The internet has opened the gate for corruption to spread into administrative positions. The accuracy of information will always be questionable. If my story provides the understanding needed to make the correct decision, then I have done a good thing for many people. If it gets me fired, then at least I will be terminated with a clear conscience. I will continue to write memoirs because I have too. I have to write down every single day of my life because I choose to walk a righteous path among wolves who are unable to stop behaviors counterproductive to the postal service.

I read out loud to the management team sections of *Federal Rules of Evidence*, Michigan Legal Publishing Ltd.

I verbalize the various punishments that would come if ever convicted. There is no fear anymore. Our office is immaculate, and they are uninvolved and perform repetitive tasks just like the contractual employees. There's no growth or plans moving forward because they do not know how to be leaders. The lead sales and service associates are in charge. They are intelligent and protected by the union. If ever crossed by a postmaster, they will administratively sabotage and wreck the financial systems needed that enables an office to stay off corporate accounting's radar. I watched Thelma do it to Jay, and it was art. I marveled at her going into my RSS, voiding all the remaining money orders. I had one left that had been chewed up by the printer. Because the customer had already paid, it created an overage in the 1412 daily financial sheet, and another money order needed to be printed. AJ retrieved another pack of one hundred, and I printed one for the customer.

Jay then had to go and adjust the overages on my 1412, which he had no idea how to do. He tried to call the RSS help desk, and when he discovered they were closed, his reply was "Sheeit." I recited the protocols for adjusting the AICs, but Jay didn't know what I was talking about. I asked Thelma.

"If Jay's not the one clearing an adjustment, who is?" I asked.

Jay very well could be a body put in a position. There is no telling how deep this goes. OIG is limited by facts and are unable to share their opinions. Furthermore, for anyone to understand, it is wishful thinking. I shared my story for public retention on an issue that needed to be resolved, at the very least on a local level. My learning continues to expand, but I wish for stability in my life.

I want to hug my son and feel his little head on my cheek and kiss him. I want to one day walk outside and feel the wind blow and smell the cedar wood in the trees. Sounds of innocents like my son's laugh or when he says "Daddy." He has autism and just this past year has started speaking.

I want to meet the love of my life and make her feel like she is the only woman in the world. I want to go to church with her, hold the door for her. Support everything that makes her happy. I want to grow old together and have no secrets. I hope I go before her, but in case I don't, I will dream about her every night until I see her again.

I have been fighting wars since I was nineteen. A stable career. That is what I yearn for.

Loading the plastic tubs inside the truck, I saw a vehicle pull inside the Newark parking lot. It was an Amazon delivery driver.

"Bernie!" I called. "Come here. I want you to look at that. Do you know what that is?"

"No, what?"

"That is a person who will work twice as hard as any employee here and for a fraction of the wage."

Five minutes later, a gentleman from Somalia came in.

"Bernie! Come here!"

I inquired with the Amazon driver once Bernie arrived, "Why did you come to America?"

"Because America...is land of opportunity," said the Amazon driver. "I can make life for myself. I give opportunity to my children." I shook his hand. "I'm happy you are here. Nice meeting you." I have nothing else to report.

United States Postal Service Employee
Joel Benner
Newark, Ohio
Sales and Service Dispatch Associate

ABOUT THE AUTHOR

Joel Benner is just a man who tries to be a good example to his son.

"Nothing in this world can take the place of persistence. Talent will not: nothing is more common than unsuccessful men with talent. Genius will not; unrewarded genius is almost a proverb. Education will not: the world is full of educated derelicts. Persistence and determination alone are omnipotent" (Calvin Coolidge).